CREATE

BRAND ATTRACTION

CREATE

BRAND ATTRACTION

A New Strategy that Uses
the Laws of Human Attraction to Decode Marketing
in a Digital and Social Media Age

MICHAEL KOTICK

ARCHWAY
PUBLISHING

Archway Publishing books may be ordered through booksellers or by contacting:

Archway Publishing
1663 Liberty Drive
Bloomington, IN 47403
www.archwaypublishing.com
1 (888) 242-5904

ISBN: 978-1-4808-4126-0 (sc)
ISBN: 978-1-4808-4127-7 (hc)
ISBN: 978-1-4808-4128-4 (e)

Library of Congress Control Number: 2017902264

Print information available on the last page.

Archway Publishing rev. date: 5/10/2017

To Ron, Nurit, and Brian, who always have
the courage to dream big with me.

Special thanks to Joe Shepter for a year of great conversation in the development of this book.

CONTENTS

LOST IN TRANSLATION

When social media first became popular, I was only a few years out of business school. My bosses at the time had come of age in a world of TVs and faxes, and like many, they found the new platforms puzzling. Why were so many people spreading so much information (and misinformation) about their brands? What could they do about it? To figure out the answer, they did what people in our profession often do when they're stumped by new technology: they found a younger person to explain it.

One of those people turned out to be me. At first, I wasn't helpful. I had grown up natively with digital technology, and it all made perfect sense to me. I was comfortable with likes and shares and letting the entire world know what I had for breakfast. As a result, my first, jargon-filled pass at explaining the brave new world was met with blank stares. I needed to explain my explanation.

I realized that I had to find a way to translate the digital experience into something anyone could understand. I first thought of explaining it with networks, but most people don't have an intuitive grasp of them. Instead, I needed something that everyone would instantly get. Luckily, at the time I was also, as were many people my age, exposed to online dating networks. I was helping friends set up profiles, chat with people they barely knew, and try to get dates. Suddenly, it struck me. *Attraction.* That would explain what was going on in a way everyone could understand.

I marched back to work and laid out the idea. I explained that in the old days, when you were looking for a date, you typically met people first and got to know them later. But in a new digital and social world, we could now go online and find out quite a bit about a person before we ever got in touch. There was even a name for this: Facebook stalking.

The same thing, I said, was happening with brands. Marketers used to be able to reach out to people through TV, but consumers would ultimately have to get their hands on a product to find out whether they liked the brand or not. Now, all that information was exposed. Anyone interested in buying something could go online and find out what our brands and products were like well before purchasing them.

Obviously, this is basic stuff today, but back then, it helped bridge the gap. They nodded their heads. They got it. And we started to talk about it and work through the problem. We could have a strategic conversation that didn't require them to hop on Facebook every day for a year first.

I never thought that explanation would be the start of anything; it just seemed like a good analogy at the time. But like many people in the digital bubble, I'm often asked about technology, especially by my parents. When my mom wants to know about the Apple Watch or Slack or why people like Tinder, I'm the first person she calls. And I've found that there is a huge gap in how she responds if I answer her in digital-speak versus attraction-speak. The former almost always gets a reply along the lines of, "But why?" If I use the latter approach and speak in the language of attraction, she invariably gets it and understands exactly why someone would want to do the things people are doing online.

For a simple example, if my mom hears me talking about "native ads," I don't try to explain programmatic buying or content marketing. I say that they are brand pickup lines. They are a quick outreach that tries to hook someone into a larger conversation. If my mom asks me why her favorite flour brand has created an online educational site about baking, I might say, "Well, you've bought their products, so they've had a few nice dates with you. Now they want to deepen the commitment." Then she understands.

The surprising thing is that this language is remarkably durable for use in describing new developments in marketing overall. By the time you're reading this, some of my examples will probably be a little stale—and some of the ones I've touted as great successes will likely be seen as passé. Nonetheless, you'll be able to use the language of attraction to explain whatever is going on. It worked in the infancy of social, it continued to work as new platforms were added, and it now works quite well for instant messaging. Whatever new technology the Musks, Zuckerbergs, and Bezoses dream up, you'll likely be able to use dating and relationship analogies to describe it.

A Method to This Madness

This should not be surprising. We often think of technology as something that has changed our lives. But we forget who made that technology in the first place. It's us. Giraffes are not out there figuring out what mobile devices and social networks should be like. Kangaroos aren't pressing "like" buttons or sharing viral videos. We (and by this I mean ordinary consumers) do this.

Whenever we use technology, we take part in shaping it. We pick the winners among apps. We provide data and information to those who are developing them. If we like a feature, we use it. If we don't, we don't—and likely share loud complaints about it in social media. In this way, we all play a vital role in the evolution of technology.

Which begs the question: what do we want technology to do? Of course, we want escape, entertainment, and education. But, believe it or not, those are all modest use cases. What we really use it for is to connect with people. We build and maintain relationships. That's why nine of the top ten mobile apps used globally are either social networks or instant messaging apps (the tenth is a game with social elements to it).[1] We chose Facebook over MySpace not because it had a superior timeline or improved shareability, but because it was better at putting us in touch with others. Today, we are flocking to WhatsApp, WeChat, and Facebook Messenger for much the same reason.

In fact, this trend is not a new one when it comes to technology—it goes way back. Since the beginning of rapid communications, we have asked it to help us with our offline social lives. In the book *The Victorian Internet*, for example, Tom

Standage devotes an entire chapter to how the telegraph fostered love, not least among those using it every day: telegraph operators. The reason is fascinating. It turns out that telegraph operator was one of the few professions in the 1800s in which women made up a large percentage of the workforce. As soon as operators started sending messages, they began to flirt over the lines. Soon, romance bloomed. Many marriages came as a result (and also a few horrifying first-and-last encounters on train platforms). Love conquers all, it seems, even in Morse code.

As technology has advanced, we have continually demanded that it allow us to reach out and connect. Online chat programs, for example, go back to the earliest days of modern computing. Instant messaging predates the Internet. Each new step has made our ability to connect more natural. Email and personal websites allowed us to attach pictures that were worth a thousand words. And who can forget Mahir Çağrı, a.k.a. the I Kiss You guy, whose lovelorn ramblings and pictures of himself playing ping-pong in a Speedo took over the Internet at one point?

If you're of a certain age, I'll bet you remember picking up an AOL startup CD at Blockbuster. Then you endured a five-minute-long, ear-piercing dialup noise—all so you could enter "a/s/l" into a chat room. (And if you're not of that age, "a/s/l" was "age, sex, location," a handy shorthand for figuring out if a connection was a possible mate.)

On the more-explicitly-about-love front, Craigslist was an early place to put text-based (and often grossly explicit) personal ads. It was surpassed by sites like Match.com, which gave you pictures and profiles. All of these were followed by

Facebook, Tinder, and Bumble. Now we have Kik, Facebook Messenger, and WhatsApp, each of which is even better at expressing emotion and building connections than traditional social networks.

In other words, a big part of the reason why the language of romance and relationships translates well to marketing activities is because of where brands are now interacting with customers: on platforms that are largely designed to support human connection.

Interestingly enough, the language translation works in the opposite direction too. For example, when I talk about romance and connection in marketing, most people's minds go directly to online dating sites. But if you think about it, such sites do not support the full scope of romantic relationships. They are merely for what marketers call *discovery*, or finding someone. A dating site is more like a search engine for people. If one matches profiles based on compatibility, it's simply a predictive marketing engine for humans, much like Amazon is for products.

Dating sites are merely the first step, and we quickly abandon them. When we make a date (or sale) with someone, we don't develop the relationship any further there. Instead, we turn to a panoply of other, richer properties to deepen the connection. A couple may meet on Tinder or Match.com, but they'll announce their relationship on Facebook, express their love through intimate talk (and maybe more) on Snapchat, and then graduate on to the Knot and the Nest. Naturally, couples are still going out to dinner and romancing each other in traditional ways, but they also use new technology developed in large part to support their journey.

That's why, for example, it's a mistake to talk about traditional and digital marketing as though they were different things. People do not have a traditional life and a digital life, they simply have appended digital technology to their own quest for deeper and better relationships. They're still doing the same things they've always done. And we should do the same.

Unfortunately, we have a tendency to obscure these facts. We prefer to hide behind highly technical language, talking about sales funnels, consideration phases, and all the rest—all of the things my parents would never understand. Sometimes these things are useful constructs, but they're occurring in a world where socialization takes precedence.

This book is about bringing that easier, simpler language of relationships into the modern conversation about marketing. We have to admit we've made marketing far too complicated. In a world that is highly fragmented and often confusing, simple terms like *pickup lines*, *first dates*, and *making commitments* can clarify and unify the different activities we're doing, no matter where they occur. Just as they did for my bosses in the early social media days, they provide a common set of concepts we can use to understand and strategize intelligently no matter what the situation.

Sources of Inspiration

To get there, however, we will need to do more than assess our personal dating history. To deepen our understanding of how brands can approach relationships, we must look at a number of different resources.

The first is the psychology of attraction. It turns out that just as people have shaped technology to support their relationships, they've also used science to understand them. If you visit any popular psychology site, for example, you'll find plenty of articles with titles like "Do Opposites Attract?" and "Why Nice Guys Finish First." These are almost always based on actual studies that have less fun titles like, "Body Image and Marital Satisfaction: Evidence for the Mediating Role of Sexual Frequency and Sexual Satisfaction." (A real page-turner, by the way.) All of these can help inform our understanding of what people really want from each other—and from brands.

In using such research, however, we have to also apply some common sense. These kinds of studies typically do not provide direct answers to marketing questions. Instead, they're examining specific interpersonal issues in carefully controlled ways. The answers they provide are often quite narrow, and their conclusions are tentative at best. An article titled "Five Ways to Make Her Say 'Yes'" usually has a level of certainty that the underlying research does not. And so, we have to balance scientific findings with what makes sense for brands.

My second source of information is one that marketers are taking more and more seriously these days: Internet stars. Throughout the last ten years, we've seen a large number of people put up videos and blog posts—and amass huge followings. In doing so, they typically pursue strategies that are highly unconventional by brand standards. In the course of this book, we'll find that these strategies are actually following the rules of personal attraction, not marketing. That makes them useful in understanding why we like some people and brands—and not others.

Finally, we'll look at brands that are either consciously or instinctively playing the attraction game right. Some of these will be well known to you, like Coke or Red Bull, but we'll also meet a range of new brands, like Herschel Supply and Yeti, that have disregarded traditional strategies and used an attraction and relationship playbook to jump right into people's consciousness.

Together, these sources of ideas and inspiration will coalesce around a simple idea: in a world where technology is developed to support relationships, brands can benefit from trying to behave like those who are successful in the attraction game. It's time we learned how to peel ourselves off the wall at the high school get-together and start asking people to dance.

Final Points

One last note to provide some orientation: psychologists tend to divide the mating game in two distinct areas. The first covers the initial phases of attraction, i.e. what makes someone seem attractive and successful in the dating game. The second phase covers longer-term attraction (or relationships). Certain traits, for example, determine whether a person would make a good life partner or simply a fling.

This book also uses that distinction. The first half largely deals with how the rules of human attractiveness can be used to help build dynamic brands. The second deals with the hard and sometimes counterintuitive work of maintaining (and deepening) relationships. There, we'll cover concepts like being there for someone, having empathy, and seeing a different angle on age-old rules and techniques to build stronger relationships with existing customers.

So let's get started. At the very least, you should find the following pages useful in understanding why we like some people and not others. At best, we'll uncover solid strategies for making sense of our fast-moving and too often confusing marketing world.

PART 1

INITIAL ATTRACTION

WANT TO FIND A MATE? SHORT OF AN ARRANGED MAR-
riage, every animal on the planet, including you, has to attract
someone. For some, it's quite simple. Male woodpeckers drum
on trees (or the side of a house if it's handy). Prairie chickens
do an elaborate dance. But sloths are probably the best. They
scream at each other, which seems strange until you remember
how many married couples do the same thing, though not for
the same reason.

Human attraction, of course, is not as simple as displaying
a great set of plumage. If we want to find mates or friends, we
can't merely be good-looking or rich. Plenty of rich people are
lonely, and lots of good-looking people can't get past the first
date. Instead, we have to be someone people like, find interesting, and want to spend time with.

Interestingly enough, the same rules apply to brands. We
know that some brands seem magnetic. Almost without effort,
they attract legions of fans across generations. Just by owning
their products, we show ourselves to be hip, cool, and interesting. This is easier for some brands than for others. If you sell
canned peanuts, you may have a small, devoted following, but

it's unlikely that you'll ever get to the iconic status of an Apple or Nike. But that doesn't matter. Just as all people have things they can do to improve their chances at the mating game, brands always have opportunities to improve their initial attractiveness.

Essentially, this involves everything from mastering the pickup line to building a strong, confident identity that your company can wear with pride. To see how your brand can get started, let's begin with that most dramatic of psychological events: an intervention.

CHAPTER 1

LET'S TAKE A HARD LOOK IN THE MIRROR

Key Takeaway

SIDETRACKED BY METRICS AND A PAINT-BY-NUMBERS AP-proach to the digital landscape, many brands have lost confidence. They think the problem is digital and social media platforms, but it's really within themselves. They need to take a look inside so they can build new, confident identities that are ready for any challenge and naturally flow from platform to platform.

Introduction

If you're like 99 percent of marketers today, you're probably a little worried. Your financials may be in good shape, and your metrics may be similar to last year's, but in the back of your mind, you know something isn't clicking. You know that somehow you're not quite connecting with your consumers as you once did. You see brands like Nike or Coke that just seem to have a knack for getting into its people's heads. But you're not there yet.

By the end of this chapter, I hope to convince you that the problem is that you're not behaving in a way that's attractive to people. The efforts you're making are most likely artificial and wooden. You're that guy at the party who is always interjecting an awkward statement here and there while conversation flows blithely around him. Let's try to zero in on what's going on.

Bob's Guide to Marketing

Imagine someone that you've known your whole life. We'll call him Bob. He's pretty much a loser. (Sorry, Bob.) He spends an enormous amount of time on the Internet and social media. He has his own website, filled with content mostly about himself. He is on almost every possible digital platform, also posting things that are mostly about himself.

Bob is also insecure. In the early days of Facebook, he was practically begging people to like him. Now if people mention him in a post, he immediately thanks them. He jumps on any trending topic or event. He posts on National Doughnut Day. He knows when it's National Umbrella Day (that's February 10, in case you're interested). During the Super Bowl, he tries to make funny comments about the game or the commercials, which is weird because he doesn't normally follow sports. Occasionally, he says something offensive and then immediately falls all over himself with apologies. All in all, he's hard to like.

He's also like many of the brands you know. If we're being honest with ourselves as marketers, we're no strangers to a tweet on National Tip Your Hat Day (January 15). We jump nervously onto every new platform (often by reposting things we've already posted on some other platform, even though they don't really seem to fit). We tend to respond to everything anyone posts about us. And way too many of us have spent the Super Bowl trying to think up something funny to say—a practice that thankfully seems to be fading in popularity.

That said, whenever we see reports that show low engagement or realize that we are not able to connect our efforts to a meaningful difference in our business, we never discuss it in normal, human terms. Instead, we have a have a rich vocabulary that covers all kinds of possible issues. We talk about engagement, influencers, CTRs, and CPMs. We follow an impossibly complex set of rules. We know that Facebook posts are more effective at forty characters than four hundred; that a blog post is most effective at 1,600 words (believe it or not, that's actually a widely recommended best practice, even though it seems awfully long);[2] and that people respond well to smiles and won't wait more than a few seconds for someone to start talking in a video.

But if a *person* came to you wondering why he or she wasn't getting much traction on social media or finding much romance on a dating site, the last thing you'd do is look at the word length of his or her posts. You wouldn't concern yourself at all with engagement rates or the list of rules that marketers have created. Those things, we know, don't really matter if there are deeper issues causing the problem. All that is just surface detail. People don't fail at social media because they're not following a set of rules, no matter what our research says. They fail because they are not interesting or likable. The same thing, of course, goes for brands. You can follow all the rules you want, but no one is going to like you if you're not likable to begin with.

To help Bob, you'd have to take a step back and say, "Let me read what you're posting." Then you'd get right to the heart of the matter. He's a bore. He's a phony. Worst of all, he's insecure. You'd tell Bob that he's better than this. He needs to be himself, get a point of view, and act with a lot more confidence. He needs to find his mojo and stop acting like a spineless toad. Or at least get a dog. That always helps.

The Anti-Bob

Now let's look at a different person, one who is much more successful than Bob online and also acts quite differently from most brands. Her name is Hannah Hart, and a few years ago, she was drinking wine (a favorite pastime of hers) and playing around with a webcam in her sister's kitchen. She was not much of a cook but had the exceedingly rare talent of being able to stay funny while completely over-served with alcohol.

That night, she taped an episode of a fictional show called *My Drunk Kitchen*. The video opened with her wearing a beanie and squinting into the camera (according to our rulebook, it took far too long for her to say anything). "This is a bottle of wine I found in my sister's kitchen," she finally slurred, "and it's free." The rest of her presentation was kinetic and fun. She ran, danced, and joked, all the while demonstrating how to make a grilled cheese—or actually, a grilled bread, since she'd forgotten to buy cheese. Finally, she wrapped up by saying, "And on a serious note, don't beat your kids."

Within a few days, her video had gotten one hundred thousand views. Within months, she had quit her day job as a translator and started making YouTube videos full-time. Since then, she has written a best-selling book and built an audience of nearly two million fanatical YouTube subscribers. They love her so much that they banded together and coughed up $200,000 on Indiegogo so she could travel around the globe to meet them all.[3]

You probably think she is successful because she's so funny, and of course that's part of it. Then again, lots of people are funny, and many are funnier than she. But if you analyze Hart carefully, you'll notice there's a method to her madness—and it's different from how brands tend to work. For example:

- She's warm and confident, while most brands are cautious and careful.
- She doesn't care what people think.
- She's funny but turns it off from time to time.
- She never begs people to like her or follow her.
- She routinely exceeds the three-minute video length considered best practices by market research.
- Forget forty characters on Facebook. There are shorter novels than her Facebook posts.
- She doesn't comment on cultural or breaking-news events (except for LGBT causes, for which she's an advocate).
- She never apologizes for offending someone.

Another way of putting it is that Hart is acting natural. She does what she thinks works. She's not the most hilarious person around, but she projects an attractive presence that makes people like her. While she's far from a traditional beauty, her comment threads are filled with people declaring their love for her and begging to be her friend. And she has done all this while breaking many of our rules. Brands should find this interesting.

Technological Insecurity

Whenever I bring up the contrast between Hart and brands in marketing circles, I typically get a blank stare. People have all but put a hand on my forehead and asked me if I was feeling well. If they bother to object, they say that it doesn't matter. They go on to say that Hannah does not act like a brand, because she's not a brand. Brands and people are entirely separate things and follow different rules—the comparison is completely irrelevant. Right?

I'll agree with the first part of that sentence, but certainly not the second. Our typical rules for brands may conform with our research, but they're problematic. Just as we can't simply look at the length of Bob's posts, there may be a much deeper reason for our shortcomings than those that we're looking at. In fact, we have to remember that we don't get to make the rules. The ones that we have created for ourselves are false, because we've limited ourselves to looking at what works (and doesn't work) for *us*, not the universe. This is an important distinction.

In the preface, we saw how people help select and change the digital platforms that become successful. Now we have to look at what they do when they're on those platforms. They're not merely using the functionality that has been provided by the app's developers, they're also setting behavioral expectations. You can think of this as the difference, say, between laws and customs. While many things are not illegal, they are frowned upon.

In extreme cases, people decide to use a platform for what they think it's good for, even if that's completely different from what the people inventing the service had in mind. The founders of Twitter, for example, thought the platform would be good for chatting and Facebook-style status updates.[4] But overall, people have decided to use it much more as an information-distribution network. On another amusing and possibly romantic note, the founders of Snapchat probably did not think of sexting when they built the app, but users quickly did.

The inmates rule these asylums, and that has consequences. Users generate one third of the content people see today, around as much as traditional entertainment media.[5] And that only goes for formal content, like videos and blog posts. It doesn't account for texts, messages, and status updates. In fact, only a tiny fraction of what people watch or read is created by brands, and much of that is paid media, which tends to be passively viewed.

Ordinary people are playing the dominant role in setting the behavioral expectations for what we do on platforms. They prefer Hannah over Bob, and for obvious reasons. She's behaving in an attractive way, while brands are acting insecurely. And it shows in our respective successes and failures.

So why are so many brands wishy-washy in the face of digital media? After all, it wasn't always this way. Back in the

Mad Men era, we used to be bold and confident, trumpeting our virtues in magazines and on television sets. We knew the media and we knew the rules, although they were highly limited in scope.

But over the last seven years or so, digital and social (and even more so mobile) have brought massive changes to our world. We've gone from a place where we had a good idea of where our customers were and how to reach them to one where the opposite is often true. People are streaming movies, cutting cords, blocking ads, and spending inordinate amounts of time watching other people play video games. Sometimes we stop and ask ourselves why anyone would want to watch someone else playing a game.

We have not had time to process what it all means. Most of us have just been playing catch-up with technology and customers. About every few months, we learn, perhaps, that our customers are spending 20 percent of their screen time watching short videos of cats doing calisthenics on YouTube. So we hire a couple of cats, teach them to do push-ups, and start creating lots of content for YouTube. But then something happens. Halfway through our new marketing program, our customers—who are always right but not always easy to please—decide that they don't like cat videos so much anymore. They want Snapchat cartoons that are 100 percent animal-free. Back to the drawing board.

We are no longer living in the forty years or so where TV commercials made our lives easy. We have new platforms where it's hard enough to figure out what people are doing and what will work for them, let alone craft experiences that break through the clutter of their lives. And the increasingly connected nature of the platforms is challenging us anew. Platforms have become more and more personal, and most social networks are making it difficult to reach our fans organically.

The good news is, this rapid change has built up our skill sets. We knew we needed to get on all of these new platforms, and we did. As a result, we all became good at moving from place to place. We can limbo messages under the various character limits for social platforms. We've mastered the fine art of responding to events in real time without offending half our audience. We're okay with notifications. And if someone came up with a site that required us to create 43.5-second videos that contained ten words of text, we'd figure it out. The real question is: with everyone now good at the basics, how do we evolve to make our brands stand out?

The Attractive Brand

The first step is to admit we have a confidence problem. We would never be reading so many articles on emerging technology and communications platforms if in the back our minds we weren't a little afraid of getting left behind. With all that going on, no one is informed enough and no one's strategy ever completely accounts for what's to come. This is a core problem for everyone. And it's driving a lot of insecurity and unattractiveness.

So what is brand attractiveness? Of course, it's not exactly the same as human attractiveness. It's more about attitude and identity. It's about understanding that we need to transform our brands into something that people care about and want to see more of, no matter where they encounter us. It's about discovering who we are, making sure we're different, and acting in a way that gets people engaged.

While brand attractiveness sounds like a radical new idea, I don't think I'm proposing anything that's all that new to marketing strategy. The term just names and isolates an approach that is being applied so far, usually in a half-in/half-out way. Obviously some brands do better than others, and a few are already in a good place.

To name one (and provide a peek into the attitude of an attractive brand), Red Bull has probably the most distinct and pound-for-pound successful brand presence in the digital world. It's not difficult to see why. The brand does extreme sports—and especially nonprofessional underground ones. It does drainage canal skating. It does urban exploring. It does big-wave surfing. It does skydiving, wingsuits, and extreme soapbox derby (yes, that's a thing). It knows edgy music. It seeks out interesting stories, like the history of skateboarding in Iron Curtain Finland or extreme sports in Madagascar. This may not be your cup of tea, but then again, no one doing all that stuff is drinking tea anyway. They're drinking Red Bull.

The brand talks, too—exactly like a person imbued with that culture. For example, every year it sponsors a particularly extreme piece of lunacy called the Red Bull Hare Run. In it, a far too large number of motorcycle racers (five hundred) speed around a muddy course covered with rocks, logs, water hazards, and discarded bikes. Typically, only twenty or so even finish.

Announcing it, Red Bull has referred to it as "hardcore carnage." That's pitch perfect.

How can Red Bull do this? A few reasons:

- **It knows who it is.** Red Bull doesn't care what Coke and Pepsi are doing. Like Hannah Hart, it is itself, and it's happy with who it is.
- **It has a unique perspective.** For a brand, anyway. Red Bull does extreme sports in its own very real way. It doesn't bother with things that are unrelated or uninteresting.
- **It's doing what it believes.** The brand lives by its code. Its strong identity naturally suggests content for it to create and support. Red Bull isn't merely in the extreme sports community either. With many of its activities, like Felix Baumgartner's skydive from 100,000 feet, it's leading that community.

Put simply, Red Bull does not really act like a brand. It doesn't care about our rules, however correct they may be from a data-driven standpoint. Instead, it looks at the larger picture of what works *in general* in the new landscape. It then goes forth and projects a distinct and confident identity.

Of course, you could point out that this hasn't led to outsized financial success. Red Bull, like all soft drinks, is in a cyclical decline. It's perceived as unhealthy in a world that's increasingly concerned with health. But in this case, its marketing may provide an exit strategy. The brand has opened its own channel on Apple's platform and is being approached by other brands with sponsorship offers and other revenue opportunities. In other words, its content has proved so effective that it may become a major revenue-generator for the company.

What's Next?

In this chapter, we've come face-to-face with a fact we can't ignore: most brands just aren't very attractive. They're too insecure to step out into the club and chat up their new life partner. Don't despair or get down on yourself—it's been a rough few years. Nonetheless, we have to admit that we have a problem, one that's not solved by our new rules or by new tactics for new platforms. Those are stopgap, paint-by-numbers measures. Instead, we need to look into ourselves, see who we are, learn to build a confident identity, and know where we're going.

To do that, let's start with the most daunting aspect of attraction: mastering the pickup line.

CHAPTER 2

THE MARKETING PICKUP ARTIST

Key Takeaway

WE CAN GAIN CLARITY AROUND MOST INITIAL BRAND communications by seeing them for what they are: pickup lines. Ads, posts, and most communications are simply there to attract customers—and most brands are pretty good at them. However, the best brands go deeper; they, like anyone successful at love, know that you must plan and own the moment after, too.

Introduction

What's the first step in starting a relationship with a person you don't know? A pickup line. Whether it's cheesy or direct, you always have to say something. In this chapter, we'll see how many brands have already gotten pickup lines right. They can grab attention. They can attract followers. They can make people smile.

But something is missing: the next step. We can't just have a pleasant, bubbly, disconnected, pickup-line-hurling, multiple-personality-complex presence online. We have to evolve into something that matters to people. So let's dive deep into how to create pickup lines, how to use them, and why they matter a lot less than we think.

The Best Brand Pickup Line Ever

What's the first thing you did when you stepped out in the dating world? Like Charlie Brown, you probably walked up to the redheaded girl (or boy) and said something terribly awkward. Then you froze up and pretended nothing had happened. Your soul was destroyed, your dreams were dashed, and your life was momentarily over. That was your first pickup line.

Brands initially struggled with pickup lines too. A few years ago, you could find them lurching from disaster to online disaster. Kenneth Cole, for example, made lighthearted comments linking footwear to alarming developments in the Middle East. Twice. Eventually, they learned that when a serious situation arises and politicians talking about putting "boots on the ground," it's not a good idea to make a joke about pumps and loafers. [6]

Other brands have dropped the F-bomb or talked about getting over-served. Today, we're mostly beyond that. Some brands have even become extremely good at this. So let's start with a story about the greatest marketing pickup line ever (and see why it didn't do much good).

It began in early 2013, when fifteen people gathered in an

office in the Tribeca neighborhood of New York City. They included executives and top creatives from the Oreo brand and all of its agencies, and they were about to watch the Super Bowl together.

This may seem, at best, an unusual way to enjoy the game, but Oreo had a plan. For months, its teams had been practicing what people were beginning to call *real-time marketing*, or commenting on current events as they unfolded. In plain English, the brand had styled cookies based on breaking news and current topics. On International Talk Like a Pirate Day, for example, they gave one an eye patch. It was cute.

The Super Bowl that year took place in New Orleans, which was a controversial choice, because the city was still recovering from Hurricane Katrina. The stadium where the game was played had served as a shelter during the disaster and become a symbol of human displacement and questionable governmental response. Not exactly an uplifting location. It got worse. During the third quarter, an electrical relay, which was ironically designed to prevent blackouts, malfunctioned and sent the stadium into partial darkness for thirty minutes.[7]

Back in New York, the Oreo team sprang into action. Within moments, an image of a cookie appeared in its Twitter feed with the line, "You can still dunk in the dark." Retweeted more than 10,000 times in the first hour, it eventually earned 525,000,000 impressions around the world. Oreo, *Wired* declared, had won the Marketing Super Bowl.[8]

Since then, many marketers have wished it hadn't. Every year, thousands of them are now forced to watch the game at work, where their bosses hope they'll make some witty come-on that spurs millions to interact with their brand. None have come close to matching Oreo's success.

The Pickup Line

When discussing efforts like this, we often like to put them in categories that make them seem much more solid, important, and technical than they really are. For example, we use *real-time* to describe a tweet during an event and *native* to describe an article we pay to put in a user's feed. Terminology like this is useful in justifying budgets or outlining strategy, but it also has a negative effect. It makes things that should be familiar to us unfamiliar. It rips us away from simple truths (like "We're just trying to make people like us") into a world where real-time and native are arcane topics that have only been mastered by the few. We read articles about them, look at case studies, and learn best practices.

Ordinary people, of course, don't see it that way at all. They don't particularly care if you're responding in the moment or have planned your tweet for months. They want to be amused or fascinated by what you have to say. They want to laugh. They want you to be interesting.

From a relationship standpoint, Oreo's tweet was simply a pickup line. It was a first conversational step in meeting the brand. We've all eaten the cookies, but we've never talked to an Oreo (except perhaps in college very late at night). Oreo has never talked to us. That tweet was its entrée into our lives, and whatever 525,000,000 impressions actually means, a lot of people read about it.

Pickup lines are a topic of some fascination. Most people find it daunting to approach someone they've never spoken to before and about whom they know nothing beyond what looks and posture can tell them. Being able to master the pickup line with the opposite sex used to be more important than it is in today's digital dating world, but we still admire those people who can easily enter into conversation with perfect strangers.

Not surprisingly, psychologists have spent a lot of time studying whether pickup lines actually work. The experiments are fun, ranging from surveys to real-world observation where researchers hang out in bars and send their grad students to try out different lines on unsuspecting people. (One of the things that I have learned about psychology is that being a grad student in that field can be an uncomfortable experience.)

Of course, the research is not settled, but in general it seems that your success or failure depends a lot on what kind of pickup line you use. Overall, we can find three major types:

- **Direct.** These are simple, honest, straightforward openings, such as "You seem nice. I'd like to get to know you."
- **Innocuous.** These are lines that could be pickup lines or not, but are more generic and nonthreatening. "Is that the new Apple Watch? How do you like it?"
- **Cheesy.** These need no introduction. They're things like, "You must have been in the Boy Scouts, because you've tied my heart in a knot." Or "Are you from Perfect, Tennessee? You're the only perfect ten I see." (Okay, I'll stop.)

Not that you need someone to tell you this, but research has shown that cheesy lines tend not to work, at least not in person. The reason seems to be that they come off as disingenuous. We tend to be fearful of new people (this goes back to our hunter and gatherer days), and a cheesy approach lacks transparency.[9] The best in-person pickup lines, believe it or not, are direct. They tend to show honesty, interest, and confidence. Slightly less effective are the innocuous ones, because they can make you seem a little timid or uninterested.[10]

So why does something like the Oreo tweet work so well? First off, it is direct. In addition, while cheesiness and canned pickup lines can be a problem, original humor falls into a bonus category. Not that we need science to tell us this, but, like confidence, it's often considered a luxury that goes a long way to making a pickup line successful.[11]

How to Test Pickup Lines

Not sure if your brand pickup lines are doing any good? There's an easy way to figure it out. Simply ask yourself how you'd feel saying that line to someone else. If your line feels awkward or ridiculous, there's probably a good reason why.

For example, in the last chapter, we discussed the current fad among brands to create messages for unofficial holidays. Most countries have only a few real holidays, but trade associations and others have declared nearly every single day of the year their own. Some are of respected heritage—believe it or not, National Doughnut Day honors the Salvation Army volunteers who served food to soldiers in World War I. But most are frivolous and recent, and almost no one observes them.

These alleged holidays really don't work for brands either. Here's why: Imagine you walked up to someone out of the blue and started talking about National Hat Day. They'd probably think you were missing a few cards from your deck. It would seem terribly weird. You'd never do it unless you were forced. And brands should not do it either. Your own impressions of how you'd feel turns out to be a pretty good litmus for brand pickup lines. If you'd say it in your personal feed, it could very well work in a brand feed. If it feels terribly awkward, it's probably not very good.

Multiple Pickup Line Syndrome

Back to Oreo. Did the tweet do any lasting good? The answer is "Probably not." A year after Oreo's epic tweet, its parent company Mondelez faced rising costs of raw materials and was forced to raise prices. In the face of this development, its customers fled. Sales cratered and never recovered. Obviously, many factors beyond marketing can affect things, but as good as the company's real-time marketing was, it did not give Oreo major pricing power.[12]

Many brands do pickup lines well, but the sad truth is that they don't matter all that much. In the first place, they're not that important in the grand scheme of things. Try to remember the pickup line you used on your significant other (or he or she used on you). You probably won't be able to recall it. That's because you don't fall in love with a pickup line. You fall in love with a person.

A bigger problem is that pickup lines work once. If you continue to use a long string of them, they wear out their welcome. For example, let's imagine that a person goes up to another person in a bar and lays out a long string of pickup lines. The conversation might go like this:

> **Brian:** Hey, tie your shoes! I don't want you falling for anyone else.
>
> **Stacy:** Um, that's funny.
>
> **Brian:** Excuse me, your eyes are blue, like the ocean. And baby, I'm lost at sea.
>
> **Stacy:** I'm sorry, I suddenly remembered I forgot my sunglasses far away from here (and you). I have to go.
>
> **Brian:** Too bad, I can't hold on. I've fallen for you.
>
> **Stacy:** Okay, I'm really going to go stick my head in a beehive now so I don't have to listen to you anymore.

While people are unlikely to do this, this is the approach we often find brands taking. They set up communications guidelines and then follow them to the letter, often trying to be playful and amusing all the time in ways that are related to their positioning. Each tweet, post, comment, or reply sounds fine by itself. But reading them all in succession is usually an exercise in madness.

To prove this, I went out on a day at random and selected twenty-four hours or so of tweets from three major brands: one technology, one soft drink, and one toilet paper. They can remain anonymous, but I deliberately chose respected brands so that you can see how even the best need to evolve.

SoftDrink	TechCo	TP
Summer is for tank tops, sunglasses, and SoftDrink.	Our CIO has been honored by @ SVbizjournal with the Judges' Choice Award as a leading CIO. Congrats!	We'll be using our #LeapSecond to take some extra time composing a #tweetfromtheseat - what will you do with yours?
Take a 20oz for a stroll in the park. #GoodTimes	Forget the grass court, the Royal Family is boosting #Wimbledon's buzz this year:	Our huge roll lasts long enough for you and your tot.
Put your ear close to the screen ... #RealSoftDrinksKnow #SoundOfSummer	You're fishing with a net when you need a spear. It's time to stop marketing to the masses:	#TweetFromTheSeat
There is no try, there is only drinking the SoftDrink.	Don't worry about being like everyone else, just focus on being the most effective you:	We support and respect everyone's right to be who they are. #LoveWins #LoveHasNoLabels #PrideMonth2015

SoftDrink	TechCo	TP
Any friend of SoftDrink is a friend indeed. #BestFriends #SoftDrinkLove	The campaign doesn't end at launch. Marketing strategies for your campaign's afterlife:	In other words … enjoy the go #TPGoesEmoji
If you couldn't make it to #TimesSquare, you can still have a shot at the spotlight. Details here: \<link\>	Geometry can be a strange and beautiful thing. A psychedelic series by @artist	A TP-filled mattress? Now that's a dream life.
We had a blast today in #TimesSquare. Thanks to everyone who tested their #OneofaKindLipSync skills.		Are you #TeamOver or #TeamUnder? #AskARandomQuestion

The tweets have no rhyme or reason to them. SoftDrink is trying to be clever all the time. TechCo has multiple personalities. TP is predictably uncomfortable to read.

On the day I collected these tweets, a victory seems to have been scored for same-sex marriage rights, which two of the brands opportunistically applauded (needless to say, we all look to toilet paper for positive social commentary, right?). A leap second was also added to the calendar, and TP urged us to tweet on the potty about it—why? SoftDrink had a lip sync contest. TechCo told you to fish with a spear rather than a net, which seems like a bad idea. TP went on about a mattress filled with toilet paper, which seems like an even worse idea. None of them is starting or continuing a passionate conversation. They are only making shallow comments that go nowhere—one right after another.

Obviously, the greatest danger in deploying a pickup line is that you don't know what to say next. If you don't have some conversation topics in mind, you're going to find yourself flat-footed. This is a fact that nearly every young person becomes aware of quite early in their dating life. By themselves, pickup lines may reflect a brand's positioning perfectly. Nonetheless, they will not create interest or a following of any kind.

Owning the Moment After

Okay, enough criticism. Let's meet some people who get this right. If you don't know what a Nerdfighter is, or you've never urged someone to "Be Awesome," you're probably not young, interested in technology, or a passionate fan of the Vlogbrothers. This YouTube channel, run by John and Hank Green, is easily one of the most successful and extensive online brands in the world today.

The two began Vlogbrothers about six years ago as a twice-a-week YouTube show. Each took on a different day by himself (they live in different cities). They talked about topics they cared about: life, technology, altruism, honey badgers, and more. Their purpose, as Hank put it, was "to try to do awesome things and have a good time and fight against world suck."

While they had quick success picking up fans, they did not stop there. They soon branched out into new things. They created ways for their followers to meet up and get involved, which led to the founding of a loose organization called Nerdfighteria.

They even launched the Foundation to Decrease World Suck, which donates money to worthy causes.

They listened, too. You've probably heard of *The Fault in Our Stars*, which was a novel and then a major motion picture about two terminally ill lovers. What you probably don't know is that it was originally a Nerdfighter project. Nerdfighteria became obsessed with the real-life story behind it and urged John, who had already written several novels, to write about it. He took up their suggestion, and the rest is history.

The Vlogbrothers aren't just about doing what they want. They don't merely put out a bunch of pickup lines. They started with something similar to that, but they had a trajectory in mind. They had a more distinct identity that could give rise and direction to additional compatible content—and indeed an entire movement. Their pickup lines were a means to an end.

Once they got to that end, they knew what to do. They listened to what their audience wanted. They didn't just sell themselves, they did things that would impact their audience. Because their Nerdfighters loved a particular story, John wrote a book and grew their content brand and offerings. He sold it and made a ton of money. Done.

Another way of putting it is that the Vlogbrothers own the moment after. They know how to attract people not merely by being interesting and funny but also by transforming that into an enduring, lasting relationship that adds meaning in their followers' lives.[13]

What's Next?

Thinking about most brand activity as pickup lines provides a great way to cut through the clutter of platforms and media strategies, and to see those communications in a simple way. We can take a few things away from this. First, it's best to be direct, warm, and authentic, though humor is always a bonus. More importantly, pickup lines are a limited tool and not a strategy, and they can backfire if we aren't ready for the next step. Successful brands are much deeper emotionally and should actively prepare for the moment after.

In the next chapter, I'll outline how you can move beyond pickup lines and create a much stronger identity and a much more purposeful program for action.

CHAPTER 3

BUILDING BRAND ESTEEM: SEIZING THE MOMENT AFTER

Key Takeaway

BRANDS TODAY NEED TO BUILD UP THEIR BRAND-ESTEEM. Much like self-esteem, *brand-esteem* means that you not only have to know who you are, you have to like who you are. There are three major ingredients to creating a strong sense of brand-esteem: building a strong identity, ensuring you are unique to others, and harnessing courage to act with conviction.

Introduction

At a fun moment in the movie *Swingers*, Trent (Vince Vaughn) decides to give some heartfelt advice on attractiveness to his downtrodden friend Mike (Jon Favreau):

I don't want you to be the guy in the PG-13 movie everyone's really hoping makes it happen. I want you to be like the guy in the rated R movie, you know, the guy you're not sure whether or not you like yet. You're not sure where he's coming from. Okay? You're a bad man. You're a bad man, Mikey. You're a bad man, bad man.

Swingers is a movie about Mike's struggle with self-esteem. In the beginning of the movie, he gets dumped by his girlfriend, which murders his confidence. Though he's a good-looking guy, he doesn't know who he is, fumbles around trying to be someone else, and generally blows it whenever he has a chance to meet someone new. In the scene above, Trent tries to build him up and get him started down the path of believing in himself again.

Trent has no such problem. He exudes the self-assurance of a player. He has no issue with who he is. He doesn't brood on his failings but instead focuses his energy on future romance. He's as skilled at meeting potential girlfriends as Mike is at driving them away. And, of course, when Mike finally regains his confidence, he too gets the girl.

The Moment After

As we saw in the last chapter, brands have to start moving beyond the initial pickup-line stage. We can no longer simply be pleasant, bubbly, disconnected, and ultimately incoherent. We know we have to own the moment after, too. To do so, we're going to have to figure out how to act in the coolly coherent, confident, and attractive way that the Vlogbrothers do—and not in the needy, pickup-line-crazed way we often resort to. We are going to have to figure out who we are, how we're different, and how to act and react in the real world. We need to be confident.

Research has consistently shown that confident people are seen as much more attractive than meek and self-doubting ones. One of my favorite studies, for example, showed that an average-looking person who is confident enough to ask another single person out will get a date nearly 50 percent of the time.[14]

We also love confident brands. There's something about a company that boldly stands for something or champions its long tradition of success. Of course, only a few brands are there right now, and to join that list, we have to go through a process that gets our mojo back. For this, brands will need to exhibit brand-esteem.

When I talk about the elements of brand-esteem, I often use an equation:

BRAND ESTEEM = STRONG IDENTITY + UNIQUENESS + ACTING WITH CONVICTION

Brand-esteem is a combination of knowing who you are, making sure you're different in a meaningful way, and acting on what you believe. All of these are essential to being attractive in today's marketplace. A strong identity doesn't help if it's the same as your competitor's. Unique positioning doesn't matter if you don't act on it. Acting doesn't help if you don't know who you are. If you have all three together, you'll have the brand-esteem you need to get people's attention.

The problem? It only sounds simple. Just as people with low-self esteem often struggle with the problem for a lifetime, brand-esteem takes work.

A Rosenberg Self-Esteem Test for Brands

Want to know where your brand rates on esteem? The most widely used self-esteem test is the Rosenberg Self-Esteem Scale. (If you're concerned about your own personal state of well-being, you can find dozens of interactive versions of it online.) As a fun exercise in writing this book, I adapted the test for brands and gave it to marketing people I know at different companies. Have a look. By the way, this is informational rather than scientific, and there's no need to score yourself too carefully.

Rosenberg Self-Esteem Test for Brands

Focus	Key Brand Question			
Identity	1	I take a positive attitude toward my brand.		
		☐ Strongly Disagree	☐ Disagree	☐ Agree	☐ Strongly Agree
Identity	2	I know what it takes for people to find satisfaction with my brand.		
		☐ Strongly Disagree	☐ Disagree	☐ Agree	☐ Strongly Agree
Identity	3	I sometimes struggle to find my brand's usefulness to others.		
		☐ Strongly Disagree	☐ Disagree	☐ Agree	☐ Strongly Agree

Focus		Key Brand Question
Identity	4	At times, I think my brand is no good at all. ☐ Strongly Disagree ☐ Disagree ☐ Agree ☐ Strongly Agree
Identity	5	I feel that my brand has a number of good qualities. ☐ Strongly Disagree ☐ Disagree ☐ Agree ☐ Strongly Agree
Uniqueness	6	All in all, I struggle to understand why my brand is different from other competitors. ☐ Strongly Disagree ☐ Disagree ☐ Agree ☐ Strongly Agree
Uniqueness	7	My products are able to do things as well as other products. ☐ Strongly Disagree ☐ Disagree ☐ Agree ☐ Strongly Agree
Uniqueness	8	I feel that the products I offer people in the marketplace are of worth, at least on an equal plane with others. ☐ Strongly Disagree ☐ Disagree ☐ Agree ☐ Strongly Agree
Act with Conviction	9	I wish others would have more respect for my brand. ☐ Strongly Disagree ☐ Disagree ☐ Agree ☐ Strongly Agree
Act with Conviction	10	I feel that my brand does not have much to be proud of. ☐ Strongly Disagree ☐ Disagree ☐ Agree ☐ Strongly Agree

If many of your answers seem negative, don't worry. In my various tests with other marketers, I've found that their reactions were usually that way. Even people who worked with highly admired brands tended to have low brand-esteem. They didn't think people knew what their brand was trying to do. They weren't sure how they were different. And they certainly didn't think that their brand had a disproportionate number of things to be proud of.

This is not merely sad, it's dangerous. It leads to the kind of pickup-line marketing we're talking about. It produces a sometimes pleasant but often confusing mix of messages—and an overreaction to criticism whenever it arises.

The Cause of Weak Brand-Esteem and Identity

To build brand-esteem, we have to begin by looking at how we can use digital media in the right way to promote our own confidence. While you often hear that Instagram or Snapchat drags down the self-esteem of those who use them, that's not entirely accurate. In fact, research has shown that the effects of a digitally social world on people and brands are more mixed—and in some ways quite positive.

It turns out that the effect technology has on you depends a lot on how you use it. When you use it to learn and achieve things, for example, it's wonderful for your self-esteem. If you need to decorate a cake for your kid's birthday, for example, you can find instructional videos on YouTube, ideas on Pinterest, and even highly technical discussions on the chemistry of frosting on blogs (no, I'm not kidding). If you plow through all of that, you'll end up with a cake your child loves—and nothing makes a parent feel better than that.

Digital technology also makes us feel better through the connections we make with others. People who use Facebook, WhatsApp, or Snapchat to set up social events, connect with relatives and friends, and share their personal passions have been shown to gain a healthy psychological boost from social media. In fact, any use of technology that connects you with like-minded people seems to be beneficial. So far, so good.

The problem is that most of us use this voyeuristically. If you passively consume other people's content about themselves, you tend to get depressed, and your self-esteem dives. The reason, quite simply, is that while we all have good and bad in our lives, people tend to post only the good. For example, you've likely never seen any of the following posted on social media:

- Look, here's the whole family happily gathered for Thanksgiving. Too bad my husband has his eyes glued to the game. #SportsLoser
- Wow, I was feeling so bad about work that I just ate a whole Costco roasted chicken by myself. #ChickenoftheBoardroom
- Unfortunately, we're going to have to hold back our 5-year-old from kindergarten for a year because he still goes to the bathroom in his pants. #MasterofDisaster #NumberTwoParents
- I just realized I've eaten crackers, hummus, and turkey pepperoni for dinner ten days in a row. #SingleLife
- Check out this Vine of me striking out five times at Tuesday's softball game. #NoPromotionForMe

Instagram is probably the worst offender. Its tagline should read, "Where envy runs wild." We all know that if you look at your feed right now, you'll find someone you know on vacation posting things like, "I can't believe what great weather we're having in Reykjavik. Blue Lagoon tomorrow!" Or "Here's the new lamb tartar at Le Cirque. Sooo good!" Of course, social media isn't the place to air the mundane and depressing, but the relentless idealized positivity of it all can make us feel like our lives or brands are less interesting.

In fact, one of the leading researchers in the field, Hanna Krasnova, has identified what she calls an "envy spiral" among people who use social media. The idea is that as we self-promote, we eventually find ourselves locked in a vicious cycle designed to make us feel worse and worse.[15]

An envy spiral works like this: Let's say you have a big circle of friends online. A snowstorm hits your area. One of the moms you know takes the kids out, builds a snowman, and gathers everyone around for a picture. She posts it to Instagram with the words, "Snow day, bliss." Even though you know the kids' dad isn't in the picture because he, quite frankly, isn't in the picture, you still compare it to your own situation. Your kids are screaming and throwing icicles at each other. You wish snow days had never been invented.

Soon, it gets worse. Another friend piles on with a post with a bigger snowman with even more smiling kids (one of yours is now in timeout, the other has his tongue stuck to an icicle). Finally, someone else posts her family smiling with an entire family of snowmen. You now want to take that icicle and stick it in your eye so you never have to look at Instagram again.

As Krasnova points out, these perfect pictures of happiness are often completely divorced from reality. In a true envy spiral, people start posting false versions of their lives designed solely for competition's sake. The succession of ever-better posts makes everyone feel less worthy, less fulfilled, and so on. Self-esteem takes a nosedive, and depression results.

Not surprisingly, if you look at any major personal brand online, it will seem quite conscious of envy spirals. The most popular YouTube star in the world, for example, is a Swedish twentysomething named PewDiePie. He makes videos of himself playing video games and shouting jokes at the screen. One of the most interesting things about him is that he's an indifferent gamer at best.

Watching people play video games these days is big business, and top players can earn millions in a year. Usually, those who post videos of their games on sites like Twitch are highly skilled, and the community as a whole is largely intolerant of poor play. It's a giant envy spiral where only a handful of people are immune. But PewDiePie's followers enjoy his sense of humor and don't feel threatened by his play. He seems to be telling his followers that it's fine to be a lousy gamer, so long as you're a good person and true to yourself. It's a lesson we could all learn.

The Brand Envy Spiral

Unfortunately, brands have not advanced to PewDiePie's point. Instead, many have gotten mired in their own envy spiral. We all naturally follow other brands and see them posting gorgeous, clever shots of their products in native feeds or in paid social media and other channels. That drives us to pour money into creating even more visually spectacular content (admit it, we're just as competitive as teenage gamers). Each act of brand self-promotion triggers more brand self-promotion. And again, we take leave of our senses.

I mean that sincerely. Relatively few people engage with (or even see) organic brand posts, except in some cases on Instagram or Pinterest. As a result, much of a brand's digital and social content falls into the general realm of amusing content on the web. The largest number of people looking at it are probably those who work at other brands. Sure, every once in a while, a brand does something amazing and captures the public's eye, but in general, we're receiving no feedback or negative feedback. In a worst-case scenario, we're destroying our self-confidence and self-esteem.

What's Next?

Brands need to fireproof themselves against envy spirals. This starts with a strong identity, increases with uniqueness, and takes it home with confident action. In the next three chapters, we're going to look at each of those in turn and see how you can create step-change with your brand and start acting in a truly attractive way.

CHAPTER 4

DON'T BE AN EMPTY SUIT: BUILDING A STRONG IDENTITY

Key Takeaway

KNOW WHO YOU ARE. A STRONG IDENTITY IS THE FOUNDA-tion of attractiveness. You can build one by digging into your brand and finding either a bold vision for the future or a great legacy from the past.

Introduction

Brands have had identities for years. These often come in slickly produced brand guidebooks that are a grab bag of graphics, voice, and personality. The problem arises that when you have plenty of time to consult such a book or consider whether a message is on brand or not, that works just great. When you're responding quickly or in real time, you need something a bit more robust. You need a strong identity, one that can serve as a foundation for fast action.

This chapter will bring forward how we can divide identities into three types: legacy, visionary, and static. We'll see that the first two can provide a strong foundation for your brand moving forward, while the last can be a big problem. Let's get started.

A Strong Identity in Action

One of the easiest ways to see who really has a strong identity (and a whole lot of esteem) is to note how a person or a brand reacts when things go wrong. In the chapter on pickup lines, for example, we saw how in the early days of social media, some brands made disastrous mistakes. Let's dig into some more of those responses for a moment and see how some did poorly while another leaned on its identity and turned a disaster into pure gold.

We'll begin with StubHub. In 2012, an employee mistook the brand's social media channel for her own and called the company a "stubsucking hell hole." As with most times when something like this happened, the brand released a stiff, formal apology: "We've deleted an unauthorized tweet made from this Twitter handle. We apologize to all of our followers for the inappropriate language used." Which pretty much confirmed the place was a stubsucking hellhole.

The American Red Cross faced a similar situation and took a different route entirely. That happened when a new employee, tripped up by her unfamiliarity with the Hootsuite platform, accidentally tweeted out the following gem: "Ryan found 2 more four bottle packs of Dogfish Head's Midas Touch beer ... when we drink we do it right #gettngslizzerd."

Most brands would have panicked (see StubHub). "What's going on with the Red Cross?" we might wonder. Here we are entrusting them with our donations, and they're using the money to get "slizzerd." Call in the experts! It's a brand disaster! But instead of agonizing over it, the organization made one of the coolest replies imaginable: "We've deleted the rogue tweet but rest assured the Red Cross is sober and we've confiscated the keys."

The Internet applauded, and Dogfish Head's Midas Touch—which was the real beneficiary of the whole episode, if you think about it—agreed to donate money every time people used the hashtag #gettngslizzerd. Everyone made out okay.[16]

Naturally, the press wanted to know how the Red Cross had performed so gracefully under pressure. The organization's spokesperson put it quite simply: "We are an organization that deals with life-changing disasters and this wasn't one of them. It was just a little mistake."[17]

In other words, the Red Cross responded to the crisis by reminding everyone of its identity. It said what it was and what it did. It is an organization that deals with tornadoes, earthquakes, floods, and hurricanes, among other things. Because it knew that, an errant tweet was no big deal. All its communications team had to do was remind everyone of its purpose, and everything was fine. Needless to say, the organization did not fire the tweeter, and life went on as usual. That's what a strong identity does for you.

But Don't I Have One Already?

You might think that your brand is just like the American Red Cross. It already has a strong identity, and perhaps it does. After all, you have a logo, you have a brand promise, and you probably conduct periodic reviews in which you hone your positioning, look for unique propositions, and create additional messaging that reflects that.

The problem is that when marketers go to work, we spend eight hours straight with our brands. We take months trying to capture our promise in a single phrase or sentence. We then go to extraordinary lengths to convey that to our customers. For us, a brand promise has serious meaning. But for our customers, who spend little to no time thinking about us on a daily basis, the brand promise is at best understood in a vague way, and usually not at all. That's why we need to think beyond making a promise to owning and projecting our true identity.

Don't believe me? Take a look at the following list, and try to imagine what the brand's promise is:

- Coca-Cola
- Starbucks
- Walmart
- Honda Accord
- Arby's
- Ford

Hands? These are some of the country's more iconic and recognized brands. And yet, for all that, none of us knows that they each stand for the following (unless it's their actual tagline):

Coca-Cola	To inspire moments of optimism and uplift
Starbucks	To inspire and nurture the human spirit—one person, one cup and one neighborhood at a time.
Walmart	Save money. Live better.
Honda Accord	The One
Arby's	Good mood food
Ford	Go further.

Of course, after reading them, some strike us as right. We may think that Ford is an innovative company and know that Accord is a very popular car. But we didn't have any idea that their brand promise specifically called these things out. Then again, some of the promises sound like they're coming from left field. You didn't know Arby's was "Good mood food." You thought it was that roast beef place with the horsey sauce that you hit up when you want a change of pace. And while Walmart does help us save money, I don't think it ever occurred to anyone that it wants us to live better. It's not that you think Walmart wants you to live worse, but nothing about it conveys an aspiration for a better life.

One brand on the list, however, has managed to convey its promise well from time to time—and not by telling us directly. Instead, it embodies its essence, making its identity the inspiration and grounding force for its activities and communications rather than a phrase used as a tagline.

Coca-Cola has had many uplifting campaigns, including a wonderful one it did in Latin America. The region has a popular Friendship Day holiday, during which you're supposed to spend time with a close friend. So Coke created a "friendship machine," a vending machine whose coin slot was too high for any one person to reach. It put them in public places on the holiday. That way, friends had to lift each other up to buy a Coke, and when they did, they received two for the price of one.

The resulting video, which got over a million views, didn't need to say that Coke was inspiring moments of optimism and uplift. It created a moment of optimism and uplift (the last one quite literally). It wasn't a loose connection to a brand promise, but one that was tight, emotional, and entirely its own identity.

And guess what? The video wasn't a terribly slick production. It put forward a unique concept that highlighted and lionized what the brand believed—and did it in a way that meant something to people. Identity doesn't have to be flashy; it has to be strong. It requires us to do something much deeper than simply making a promise. This is the hardest part.

What Kind of Identity Works for You?

To have a strong identity, you have to figure out who you are and like who you are. Any successful identity has to be something you and others can look up to and be inspired by. It has to be able to live on its own. In essence, there are three types of identity: visionary, legacy, and static.

Visionary Identities Give Brands a Mission

Instead of simply making products, some brands aspire to a larger or higher calling. They are trying to do something, achieve something, or help their customers do or achieve something. They have a vision of the future that drives them forward. They're leaders of a greater cause.

Brands that have this kind of identity are usually strong and confident. Nike wants to transform you into the best athlete you can be, encapsulating that with its "Just do it" slogan and things like its "Find Your Greatness" campaign that featured ordinary people struggling to get off the couch and into shape. Coke wants to inspire you. The Red Cross also has a mission: to help people get back on their feet after disasters.

But almost any kind of brand can have a forward-looking vision. A crayon brand might want to enable children's artistic creativity, while an airline might want to unleash your inner explorer. When you have that kind of identity, you can easily gain confidence because you are working toward a purpose, not merely projecting a message or a succinctly written promise.

Legacy Identities Build Pride

The strongest heritage brands tend to have legacy identities. A legacy identity does not mean that you're always looking backward. It means you have strong roots and see yourself as carrying forward a worthy tradition.

Most of these brands are long established, like Gucci, Ford Trucks, or Wells Fargo, but even a relatively new brand like Ben and Jerry's can have a strongly rooted legacy identity. The company was founded based on being both fun and socially responsible. That identity is so important that when Unilever bought Ben and Jerry's, it was adamant in continuing its charitable work and advocacy, even though the left-leaning principles of the brand were not for all of its customers (or its new parent company). As a result, the brand kept its strong identity—one that's easy for some customers to like and helps employees find pride in their support.

Static Identities Risk Loss of Confidence

There is, of course, another kind of identity: one that neither looks forward nor backward, but is static in nature. This is probably most brands. They tend to define themselves according to what their products do. Such an identity does not necessarily kill a brand, but it's harder to love.

Static brands have little to say in the give-and-take of the digital world. Without a mission, they don't have a coherent voice or consistent subject matter. They end up talking about lip sync contests and National Feral Horse Day. Very few people care.

Strengthening Your Identity

The good news is that it's not difficult to strengthen your identity if you commit to it. Every brand has periodic reviews and rethinks its positioning or mission. You can now use those same processes but layer in a new element, one that seeks out a stronger identity. Here are some ways forward:

1. **Get inspired by what your product could achieve.**
    Only a few products have no functionality and value.
    Yours certainly does something beyond making floors
    10 percent cleaner, let's say. You need to extend that
    concept outward. Do you stand for cleaner floors, or
    do you stand for an easier life, safer children, or something more? For example, Under Armour stands for
    improving performance. Of course its clothes do that,
    but having an identity also creates a more holistic vision
    that has led the company to purchase fitness software
    and build a database that helps it provide individualized
    feedback to athletes. While it does sell clothes, it is inspired by performance, which in turn drives its success.

2. **Remember your roots.** Alternatively, it sometimes
    makes sense to pick up a book, interview the grandchildren of your founders, and dig into the archives to
    understand what the founders of your business thought
    and why they did what they did. Getting back to your
    roots can provide a powerful inspiration for a strengthened identity.

3. **Ask the five whys.** If you're like 99 percent of us, your
    initial attempts to find a purpose or legacy may not feel
    entirely inspirational. They may not point to a path
    forward for innovation or get you excited or overflowing
    with ideas. That's fine. You're on the right path; you

just need to delve deeper. One great way to do so is a technique known as the five whys. To do this, you first state your identity. Then you ask, "But why?" Answer the question and then ask it again until you find a more inspiring, confident, and even surprising identity for your brand. Typically, you will not need all five whys—one or two usually suffices—but you should soon find unique ways your brand can add value and serve a higher purpose than simply selling decent products.

4. **Make sure you can love the identity.** If you don't like your brand, no one else will. You need a brand identity that is something you believe in and care about—one that energizes you every morning, even giving you a heightened sense of purpose in your work.

5. **Be okay with (a few) haters.** If you look at any brand that has a strong identity, it has its detractors—by design, a strong identity creates a tribe of people who are in, and hopefully a much smaller number of people who are out. Don't be fearful of this or think it will threaten your business or reputation. Ben and Jerry's has faced periodic calls for boycotts from groups over its support of certain social causes. It has stuck to its guns and prospered. Haters just come with the territory.

Case Study: Vision and Legacy in Chrysler's Rebirth

Brought to the brink of bankruptcy by the 2008-2009 financial crisis and sold to Fiat, Chrysler needed a rallying point that could coalesce its people and swing public opinion in its favor. To do this, it took a journey into its legacy.

Chrysler has a long history. Many may not remember that it was originally a luxury brand from the once flourishing but now beleaguered city of Detroit. To the surprise of everyone, the brand embraced both of these aspects of its roots. At the Super Bowl in 2011, it launched a new identity with its "Imported from Detroit" commercial. Featuring rapper Eminem, the ad didn't shy away from the gritty streets of the city but rather celebrated them as the source of hard work and pride, which it saw as the foundation of quality and luxury.

The commercials immediately struck a chord, and this renewed identity had great sympathetic appeal. It was a promise to stay true to the company's roots, help the city of its birth, and uphold the great tradition of car manufacturing in the city. It took on a cause and a mission that were greater than just a car brand. In turn, sales jumped, which netted the campaign a Grand Prix at the Effie Awards, one of the few advertising contests to measure effectiveness. The new identity had great, and lasting, public appeal.

What's Next?

Put simply, marketers need to do a bit of self-examination. Very likely, their brands are a little tired and functional—and could be greatly strengthened. In your next brand discussion, try to draw inspiration from either the promise of your product or the legacy of your company to forge a stronger identity. Give your customers and employees something to trust and believe in, and you'll greatly improve the attractiveness of your brand. Above all, don't be an empty suit. Know who you are and then some.

In the next two chapters, we'll see that while a strong identity is a great starting point, to win the attractiveness game we'll also need to make sure we're differentiated and can put our plan into action.

CHAPTER 5

BE UNIQUE: STANDING OUT FROM THE CROWD

Key Takeaway

UNIQUENESS IS A KEY FACTOR IN ATTRACTIVENESS. YOU build it by bringing energy to your identity and making it strong and vital—rising above a mere set of principles. Allow your brand to stand out in a good way and give people an emotional reason to connect with you.

Introduction

Classic movies often provide a window into deep human truths, and *Good Will Hunting* is no exception. The film contains a very telling scene in which Ben Affleck and Matt Damon chat up a pair of college girls at a local bar. They are immediately interrupted by an obnoxious grad student named Clark. He snottily challenges Affleck's claim to be a history student. "I was just hoping you could give me some insight into the evolution of the market economy in the early colonies," he begins before going on a pretentious rant.

After a while, Will (Damon's 160 IQ character) steps in. His criticism is cutting and to the point as he demonstrates that Clark got all his ideas from somewhere else. He even cites books and page numbers.

"In about fifty years," Will scolds him, "you're going to start doin' some thinkin' on your own, and you're gonna come up with the fact that there are two certainties in life. One, don't do that. And two, you dropped a hundred and fifty grand on a f*ckin' education you coulda' got for a dollar fifty in late charges at the public library."

Clark snorts back, "Yeah, but I will have a degree, and you'll be serving my kids fries at a drive-through on our way to a skiing trip."

"Yeah," Will says. "Maybe. But at least I won't be unoriginal."

Needless to say, Will ends up with the girl. It's not that he's better looking (okay, maybe a little) and certainly not that his socioeconomic status is higher. Rather, he's shown himself to have a unique perspective. He is an original thinker, and that makes all the difference.

This doesn't merely go for Hollywood. Differentiation and uniqueness are key elements not only in building brand-esteem but also in attracting those passionate brand loyalists about whom we talk so much. So let's not keep it a secret.

Defining Uniqueness

If a strong identity is who a brand is, uniqueness is how it stands out. Of course, every brand is to some degree unique. But more mature brands and industries tend to have smaller differences in identity. They're like Clark. He may not have his own vision, but he likely has made a thoughtful selection of ideas that he feels differentiate him from other history majors. Those ideas may not be entirely original, but they would make his perspective ever so slightly different from others. Brands can be the same way. We all know what computer security companies do, and typically they offer slightly different benefits. But there are few clear differences between their brands and products.

Unlike Clark, Will's originality is baked into his DNA. He lives alone, presumably abandoned by his parents, in poverty. Yet he has a force of intellect that sets him completely apart from everyone—and the combination of circumstances and gifts makes him truly unique. He may be emotionally troubled, but he not only absorbs things like math but also makes stunning contributions to them. Like Will, breakout brands add energy, originality, and difference to a conversation. It's not just about being differentiated; it's about having the unique ability to add a new perspective.

To see how it works, we can start with insurance. This is one of the most competitive industries in the world, with good margins and stable, highly predictable profits. As a result, it has become a titanic battleground of advertising and branding. The brands in the category are among the best at playing in the new marketing world, and almost all make interesting, shareable content. So let's think about four of the big players: State Farm, Nationwide, Geico, and Aflac.

Nationwide and State Farm sit on one side of the divide. One of them is "on your side." The other is "there for you." If you can find a discernable difference between these positions, I'm impressed. Digging into their marketing and social feeds, you'll find that they stick to topics and speak in ways that you'd expect from insurance companies. They obviously employ skilled and talented people, and their content is often touching or amusing, but they don't set themselves apart from the rest. Close your eyes for a moment, and you'll probably think of them as staid, tired brands. They're pretty much the same.

Geico and Aflac, however, have veered in a different direction. Each has created a unique identity centered on an animal with peculiar characteristics. The Geico brand's most enduring mascot is its gecko, a Cockney-accented character who quickly steers almost any conversation to saving money with the brand. The Aflac duck, on the other hand, is restricted to a single quack, which it employs (usually in frustration) when people are discussing how difficult it is to find good insurance. Both energetically add their message—often literally—to a conversation people are having. Close your eyes again, and you'll see they seem young and fun. And that's no easy feat, because these companies aren't. Both are over fifty years old. One was founded as the Government Employees Insurance Company and the other as the American Family Life Assurance Company. They'd be right at home with the Atlantic & Pacific Tea Company.

And don't just take it from me. My favorite tool for measuring uniqueness is BAV Consulting's Brand Asset Valuator, which uses twenty years of data from close to a million people to measure the attributes of a brand. It considers "energized differentiation"—that is, uniqueness—as a core driver of brand value and pricing power (its ability to demand a premium price in the marketplace). The following chart shows the uniqueness scores for State Farm, Geico, and Aflac, and it pretty much confirms what you'd suspect from the above.

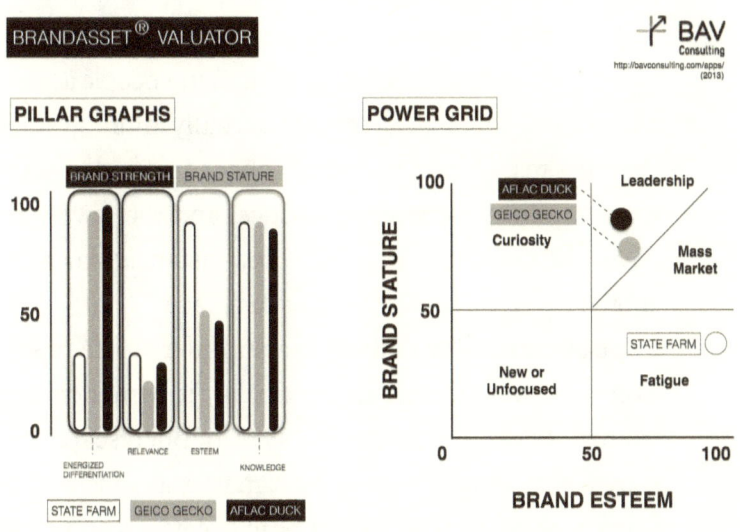

Let's Get Physical

To gain a better understanding of perceived uniqueness and why it's a critical part of attraction, let's look at how we, as people, come to the conclusion that something or someone is truly attractive. It turns out that human beings come to some very quick initial conclusions about how good-looking a person is. In fact, it takes about a fraction of a second to make that judgment.

What do we do in that second? Well, first we look at physical appearance overall, and researchers have shown that we're actually pretty hardwired about that initial assessment. In fact, we seem to base our evaluations on three things: regularity, proportion, and symmetry.[18]

- **Regularity.** Believe it or not, if you take photos of peoples' faces and average them together, the end result is better-looking than any of the individuals. Contrary to popular belief, good-looking people are not exceptional-looking. They are actually more average than the rest of us. One theory about this is that we're scanning for genetic irregularities, and the fewer you have, the better. Jessica Alba, for instance, has been shown to have a remarkably average face.[19]
- **Proportions.** Our culture has an unfortunate obsession with weight, and in particular, it demands that women strive to be unreasonably thin. But research has shown that weight itself doesn't matter as much as we think it does. In truth, size doesn't matter as much as the ratio of body-part sizes to one another. For example, Indo-Europeans across a wide geographical range prefer a .7 waist-to-hip ratio regardless of how much a woman weighs. That helps explain why a painter in Peter Paul Rubens' time, for example, found somewhat heavier women to be ideal. They are proportionally similar to today's knockouts.
- **Symmetry.** Less surprisingly, we want left sides to look like right sides, and eyes to be equidistant from noses.

There's actually a widely circulated Internet rumor that actor Denzel Washington has one of the most symmetrical faces ever studied. It does not have a basis in fact (although Denzel fans may disagree), but symmetry is nonetheless important.

In other words, while many people think of beauty as consisting of some set of qualities (blond hair, blue eyes), our snap judgments on looks are often made with sophisticated mathematical precision—and we tend to have broad agreement as a species on these things. So next time you're out with your friends, stop talking about perfect 10s and start talking about perfect .7s. That's what you're actually excited about.

What Matters More

There's more good news for all of us who aren't on the cover of fashion magazines. Raw looks matter a lot less than we think. My favorite study on this topic involved students looking at pictures of people and rating them on attractiveness. Some were generically good-looking but poorly dressed. Others were not terribly good-looking but were clean-shaven and well put-together. It turned out to be a slam dunk for clothes and grooming. So your tip for the day is to stop obsessing about your looks, get a haircut, iron your pants, and accessorize thoughtfully.

At this point, however, we do not seem to be finding much support for uniqueness. After all, we don't like unusual people—we like average people. We don't like intriguing faces—we like purely symmetrical ones. And we don't go in for super-beautiful. We like people to be clean-cut and well maintained. This all seems an argument for blandness, not originality.

Of course, we know that this must be wrong. The people (and brands) we love are not bland and generic. They're original and interesting. No one ever said, "I fell in love with Mark because I found his ordinariness a complete turn on." Or, "I love those boring ads for Level 3 Communications, whatever it is that they do." We may buy generic products, but we have no affinity for them. Their only attraction is their low cost. Differentiation is a key factor in attraction, pricing power, and everything else.

This is also true of people. It turns out that while we are hardwired and consistent in our snap judgments about physical attractiveness, over time we are wired for differentiation in overall attractiveness. Studies have shown that our opinions of others rise or fall based on their unique qualities. We may start off with the same assessment as everyone else. But as we discover someone as a person, we find unique traits that are attractive (stress-free, sports-obsessed, loves to hike) or unattractive (chews with mouth open, sports-obsessed, loves to hike).

If you look at a bunch of people in a bar, you might think that Jim, the dashing pool player with the well-pressed shirt, is the one to watch. Then, if you find out he's an obnoxious drunk with a gambling problem, his value drops considerably. Or if you learn that that average-looking dude shares your passion for the electric ukulele, his stock rises exponentially. Unique qualities shift our evaluation one way or another. A bland and undifferentiated brand may offend no one, but it also attracts no one, because it's not providing any point of real connection.[20]

We see this with personal brands as well. Everyone finds Hannah Hart funny. That's our snap judgment. However, not everyone becomes a follower or a fan. We have tons of options for entertainment, so only some of us find ourselves in such harmony with her unique perspective on life that we become passionate fans and advocates. Those of us who do see ourselves in her fall in love. The rest stop watching her, although we respect her talent.

The more time we spend with brands, the less their generic attractiveness affects us, and the more their unique qualities (or lack thereof) start to play a role. Even though being unique takes courage, it ultimately gives you a perspective and allows people to develop an affinity for you. State Farm and Nationwide may produce good content, but it's just what you'd expect from an insurance company. The brands may blanket us with advertising, but they're fatigued as brands, even when they're being funny. By contrast, Aflac has its duck delivering a similar message (it is also an insurance company) but in a completely unique tone, voice, and perspective. You may just fall in love with that silly duck.

Of course, just like Ms. Hart, Aflac will never convert everyone into being a passionate admirer of the duck. However, it will convert some. Nationwide, on the other hand, has taken a much harder road.

The Fat Jew and User-Generated Content

We've established that what you communicate and how you communicate matter much more than surface qualities. What does this mean for brands? In the past ten years, we have focused a good deal of our attention on doing great creative work. We invest heavily in graphics and photo shoots—which is fine—but no matter how sexy or polished our content is, it matters a lot less than we once thought. It's much more important to position what you're communicating effectively and to have a unique outlook that can add something to the conversation.

Rather than spending millions of dollars on showy creative that reflects our positioning, we should stop and think about what and how we want to communicate. We have to be much more strategic first. We need to find our identity and uniqueness at the onset, and use it to speak confidently in a digital world.

To prove that uniqueness is an identity issue, not just a creative issue, we can look at one of the best personal brands on the Internet that doesn't make *any* creative content at all. He borrows all his visuals from other people, and it still works.

His name is Josh Ostrovsky. Better known as The Fat Jew, he is one of the world's most popular Instagramers. With a hilariously profane feed and a haircut that consists of a long topknot sticking a foot or so off the top of his head, he has little trouble standing out. Personally, he's as unique as they come.

His content, however, is not entirely his. None of it, in fact, is strictly original. Instead, he relies on memes and funny photos generated by others. Typically, he posts an already funny piece of visual content and then adds his own cynical spin.

Most of what he says is outrageous and unprintable, but as an example, he might post a picture of kids graduating high school and write, "That's right. Our parents all had sex around the same time eighteen years ago." (His version, of course, would have slightly stronger language.)

The Fat Jew manages to be unique in two ways. First, he is selective in what he chooses to post. He has themes: the futility of exercises, the wonders of pizza, dogs behaving like humans, and the sad side of humanity in general. Second, he puts his own stamp on everything, a uniquely guilty pleasure, deeply suspicious of many current sacred cows. He'll talk about white people, overweight people (he's both himself), dietary fads, and ongoing trends. While everyone was going nuts of over the Ice Bucket Challenge, for example, he wrote: "Guys, there's war around the world and Missouri is on fire, BUT DON'T WORRY BECAUSE WHITE PEOPLE ARE POURING ICE ON THEIR HEADS FOR CHARITY!" In other words, by being selective about his content selection and speaking with his own voice, he stands out in a world where so much is shared.

Building a Unique Presence

The brands that are best at creating a differentiated identity follow a similar formula. They create a series of rules and elements that serve as filters for both long-term initiatives and the quick, snack-able brand communications that are mission-critical for digital and social media today. Here's how you can get started:

1. **Begin with your identity.** In the last chapter, we discussed the importance of a strong identity in building confidence. Put simply, without going through that first step, you won't have the ability to consistently stand out.

2. **Identify the energizing characteristics that work with your brand and set you apart from your product category.** This is the tough part. The Fat Jew stands out through his cynical irreverence. But that may not work for you. Instead, you need to figure out how it is you want to connect. It may be, as with the Geico Gecko, with a Cockney accent that brings the complexity of insurance down to a simple level. But if you're a brand wanting to unleash creativity, you'll do this in a different way. Think in terms of characteristics (funny, provocative, optimistic, professorial, etc.) rather than a set of core values.

3. **Mash up your identity, your energy, and your product.** So many brands in social media run away from what they sell. Instead, you should put your product first. It is a key element in your differentiation and the way you're going to create sales—and nobody's going to be fooled into thinking you're in this for your health. Next, devise a set of appropriate strategic filters for your brand. These can be visual or stylistic, but they should ensure that you put your stamp on everything you do. And don't be afraid to use them to reject content. If someone with a large following (or high social

influence) posts something that's positive but doesn't fit your criteria, leave it off. Don't fall into the trap of selling out your unique identity for a few extra impressions—your identity is worth more than that.

4. **Inspire, don't communicate.** An old graduate-school professor used to remind me that there's a big difference between someone who says they're funny and someone who is actually funny. In the same vein, don't say that you're different, just be different. In the modern era, you'll never talk anyone into liking you. No one will take the time to master your talking points. Instead, your brand has to inspire simple emotions. Nike inspires its customers to think they can be great. Coke inspires them to feel better. Harley makes people feel like part of an elite, rebel band—but it never tells them they're part of one or why they should be.

5. **Keep your antennae up.** Categories move quickly, and competitors like to copy success. Ensure that you are always challenging yourself to push further and evolve over time. (More on this in Chapter 6.)

Case Study: Herschel Supply

One company that really gets uniqueness is Herschel Supply. As a luggage brand, it's in a crowded category, but it manages to stand out by inspiring simple, sophisticated adventure. To do this, it primarily uses photos submitted by its fans, which it carefully curates according to its own criteria. It inspires them to be creative in line with its differentiated identity and rewards them when they succeed.

Looking at a few of the posts, it's easy to see a pattern emerge:

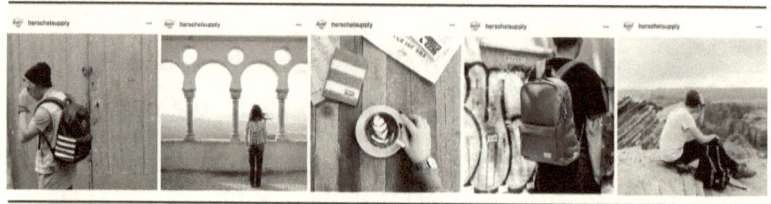

How does Herschel do this? Let's go over the steps we established above:

1. **Begin with your identity.** All of the images say one thing: Herschel Supply is about adventure with style. The pictures are understated, often with an emphasis on beautiful natural settings.

2. **Identify the energizing characteristics that work with your brand and set you apart from your product category.** It's pretty clear that Herschel Supply thinks of itself as independent. You rarely see travelers together. In addition, everyone dresses with the same simple stylishness that the brand designs into its bags. It's focused on originality, being different, and going off the beaten path. But it's not about competitive traveling or scruffy sports adventures.

3. **Mash-up your identity, your energy, and your product.** On average, about half the photos have a Herschel product. In addition, we can identify a number of strategic filters they use to choose the kinds of images they want to show. You'll never see a Herschel Supply bag next to the dumpster in a Denny's parking lot. The people using the products seem young and cool. They are always casual and relaxed—this is not a brand about conquering Denali with your last breath. These people are more likely to be looking for the perfect cup of tea or a secret spot.

4. **Inspire, don't communicate.** This one should be easy. The brand demystifies travel and makes it feel more approachable. It isn't something difficult or dirty. We see things through the traveler's eyes. We are usually looking at their backs, not their faces, which gives us the same perspective as they have. As a result, we're not seeing a smiling (and let's face it, bragging) face. We're able to contemplate the scenery just as they do, and be inspired to travel too.

Herschel Supply has created a formula that links back to what it wants to achieve. It has zeroed in on an energetically differentiated position in the market. The brand only elevates certain content that shows off a distinct persona. Users, in turn, have learned what that formula is; if they want to share in the brand, they have to take photos that are inspiring rather than boastful. Once they succeed, the brand rewards them while keeping its feed fresh and relevant to those who love it.

This approach extends further than just social media. You'll see the same differentiated identity in any marketing communication that Herschel Supply puts forward. This is just who they are.

What's Next?

If identity is who you are, uniqueness is the particular energy you bring to your mission. All brands have an opportunity to do this, and it's critical for projecting confidence and being attractive to others. Whether you use a character, curate, or provide a perspective or voice you've developed, we no longer live in an era where a bland, consistent presence can sustain a brand. If you want to be attractive, you have to put your own unique spin on things. It's that simple.

CHAPTER 6

IT'S TIME TO ACT: PUTTING YOURSELF OUT THERE

Key Takeaway

PROJECTING YOUR STRONG, UNIQUE IDENTITY REQUIRES A certain degree of faith. To succeed, brands have to be prepared to fake it till they make it. They need to launch their new attractive selves and insulate themselves from any breakdown in confidence. As we'll see, there is no psychological evidence that suggests love at first sight is a real thing. You have to be ready for the long haul and the bumps and bruises that come with it.

Introduction

The motivational speaker Dr. Ivan Joseph, who is also soccer coach at the prestigious Ryerson University in Canada, tells a great story about recruiting players. When their parents come to tryouts, he asks them why he should offer their kids a scholarship. Almost all of them respond by highlighting some aspect of their child's athletic prowess. One may be able to kick the ball a great distance. Another may have great field vision. A third could have blinding speed. But, Joseph says, none of those are the most important qualities in a soccer player. None of it matters at all, in fact, if a player lacks the self-confidence to act. You may be super-fast, but if you hesitate to get going, your speed does you no good.

Acting with conviction is the final piece of the confidence equation. It's how brands take their energized identity and put it forth into the world. True breakout brands are characterized by confident action. They believe in what they're doing and saying, and everything that comes out of them—whether it's a well-planned ad campaign or an in-the-moment reaction—seems completely natural. In this chapter, we'll see how brands can take this final step, and how, surprisingly enough, it opens up big creative possibilities.

Channeling Your Inner Rock Star

Most people think of conviction as an innate trait. People either believe in themselves or not. They are able to write or not. They are big and strong or not. Unfortunately, it only looks that way. You always have to work at it.

One of the most interesting angles on acting with conviction comes from social scientist and researcher Ruth Blatt. She made a particular study of the business, organizational, and psychological aspects of being a rock star. While we tend to think of the music business as sex- and drug-fueled hedonism, its most successful practitioners also tend to build businesses—and sometimes far-reaching brands.[21]

For every great musician brand, there are thousands of excellent musicians you've never heard of. In the marketing world, in fact, we meet lots of them. They can be found in nearly any production studio that helps with videos or commercials. They can compose the perfect score for almost any application. They have the enviable ability to pick up a guitar and play just about anything. But like Jason Segal's character, Peter, in *Forgetting Sarah Marshall*, they can't just play in that utterly calm and commanding way that makes the action seem effortless.

In fact, most people aren't born with the ability to act with conviction. Comedians almost always have to learn to shut down hecklers on open-mike nights. They have to work at their craft to get better. Most rock performers are apparently the same way. For example, Blatt points out that Prince, an epic performer, was not always one. Early on, in fact, his stage presence was so bad that Warner Bros. Records didn't even allow him to tour for his first album. Then Rick James took him on tour, and Prince made good use of the time. He studied James and other great musicians. He copied their style and incorporated moves of his own. He faked it, worked at it, and soon became not merely a serviceable performer but one of the best of all time.[22]

Learning to Brag to Yourself

Like Prince, brands who have secured a unique identity need to get it out there. To do so, they have to find ways to express that identity initially without eroding their confidence. A strong identity alone won't carry you through. Every new brand-identity venture is vulnerable, especially in the beginning. If you step out and make a few stumbles, you'll quickly find your team second-guessing itself. In this sense, people aren't very different from brands.

A commonsense example can easily show why. Imagine you're a single male, and you decide you are going to meet the mate of your dreams one night. You call up your friends and decide on going to a jazz club, where smart, sophisticated people tend to hang out.

To maximize your success, you work on your identity all day. You start the morning with a new haircut and then head to the gym. Then you find that new outfit you know looks perfect on you. You put on a generous splash of Eau de PerfectDude, and you stride confidently out the door. Finally, the coup de grâce: you enter the club, buy a martini, and start slurping down some courage. You have a transformed identity. You are a very attractive version of you.

Then what happens? You look over at your first candidate sitting with her friends at the bar. Your eyes lock, and then she gives you a look that seems to indicate that she's gazing at a particularly unappealing species of skunk. What you don't realize is that she's actually badly nearsighted, just broke her glasses, is merely trying to get a better look at you. Nonetheless, you start feeling down. So you re-up your courage with another cocktail and go try again.

Unfortunately, the object of your desire this time has just been dumped by some jerk via text message. She wants revenge on the entire world, but because the entire world isn't available, she decides you'll do as a stand-in. You retreat from this encounter feeling worthless. Your strong identity leaves you, and after a few more whiffs at the plate, you head for the door.

The truth is, if you had continued to act with conviction, these setbacks wouldn't have gotten you down. If Prince stumbled onstage, it was simply an aberration. It didn't affect the rest of his performance in any way. We all stumble, but we have to go on.

So how can you do this? The first thing to note is that you are much more likely to hear bad than good. Studies have shown that people of all demographics are much more likely to provide negative feedback to a company than positive.[23] It's just human nature. Believe it or not, there is an Apple Sucks Facebook page. Admittedly, it has only around 6,000 followers, but that's actually high as those things go (the Microsoft Sucks has only 1,200 or so).[24] So expect to face criticism. It's bound to happen—even to the best.

So how can you keep up your spirits? Try the following:

1. **Exercise strong leadership.** It's critical, of course, to have strong leadership committed to the brand identity. You cannot commit to a unique identity (whether it's a small pivot or a fundamental transformation) without leadership supporting it. If you look at the turnaround of any fading brand—be it Best Buy, Ford, or Domino's—it began with a fresh face in the captain's chair. In addition, leaders and brands can use tools and techniques to stay confident.

2. **Make a brag sheet.** Bragging to others is a problem. Bragging to yourself is healthy. To act with conviction, you need to remind yourself of everything you already do well, as well as everything that's great about your new identity. Make an argument about why your brand is better, your positioning is better, and your identity is stronger—in short, why you matter. If you're a heritage brand, lean on your history. If you have a vision, own it. Then, whenever you encounter the inevitable detractors or find setbacks, whip out that document and remember why you're doing what you're doing.

   For example, when our wannabe Lothario above went to the jazz club, he allowed his sense of self to drift. He should have arrived with his brag sheet top-of-mind and not allowed a few unlucky interactions to get him down. Whenever he was faced with setbacks, he could have said, "Wait a minute, I'm a nice guy with a decent job. I look good, and just the other day, someone told me I was a terrific catch." That would have insulated him from disappointment and kept him on track. It's the same with brands.

3. **React to feedback intelligently.** In the story above, our hero made a quick, negative determination of why he was getting shot down. In fact, the first person was actually interested in him; she was just missing her glasses. The second was reacting to the universe, not him. She would have done the same thing to Channing Tatum. Again, if someone doesn't like something about

your new identity, expect to hear about it. But try to interpret it in a positive, healthy manner. Sure, you might make a mistake, but you'll understand that you made it for a good reason and with good intentions.

4. **Fake it till you make it.** Believe it or not, one of the best ways to become the person you want to be is to start being that person. It's true. If you're in a bad mood and turn your mouth into a smile, you'll feel better. One frequently cited study forced students to hold chopsticks in their mouths in a specific way while performing stressful tasks. What they didn't realize was that the way they were holding the chopsticks forced some of them to wear smiles. (It must have been a strange afternoon for all of them.) The smiling participants came through the ordeal much more serenely.[25]

A wide range of studies support the idea that simply acting like you know what you're doing is a great strategy for doing things well.[26] Brands can certainly learn from this. Once they decide on a unique identity, they can simply start being who they want to be. You're not really faking it if you're doing it.

5. **Repetition, repetition, repetition.** You need to be able to pioneer and redefine your brand, and then stay resolute. It takes at least a year to firmly establish and own an identity, sometimes even longer. You may not get it right at first. It will take practice and time to make your new identity and uniqueness characteristics a

habit. Stick with it and have resolve. Eventually, you'll be the brand you want to be.

A final thought: remember that marketers tend to think that their short-term actions are much more important than long-term. Product matters. Most of the time, it takes a *really* off-base marketer and consistent mistakes over the long term to destroy a brand. So have a go at it, listen to feedback, improve over time, and soon you'll be living your new identity.

Case Study: Domino's

To see how this can work in the real world, look to one of the most abrupt turnarounds in recent brand history. For fifty years, Domino's was known as a brand for its amazing promptness, convenience ... and poor pizza. Like most pizza chains, it had cut costs by using inferior cheeses, substandard sauce, and cheap toppings that they heaped on the pies by the handful. Domino's, according to a study by Brand Keys in 2009, was the worst of the bunch, ranking dead last in flavor.

At the same time, the brand was confronted with a public that was growing more food-savvy. Pizza at independent restaurants across the country had improved. You could get fresh ingredients and an artisan crust in just about any city in the United States. These trends were also neatly reflected in Domino's financial results: sales were declining, and investors were restless. It seemed to be a zombie brand in the making.

At the height of the crisis in 2007, the company hired Patrick Doyle as CEO. A ten-year veteran of the company, he, like everyone on the planet, knew what the problem was. But he and his team soon coalesced around a new identity energized by unique characteristics: transparency and honesty. They would admit their pizza stunk and would work to improve it.[27]

Soon, Domino's released a remarkable series of commercials that were more akin to documentaries than promotions. They told the story of Domino's transformation and how it conducted focus groups and research to determine the problem. They highlighted the decision to start using real cheese and making a better sauce. The campaign was raw, unvarnished, and brutally up front. Nowhere did the company claim to make the best pizza. But it would make a good pizza. These actions demonstrated almost every aspect of acting with conviction.[28] In doing this, it followed all of our steps:

1. **Exercise strong leadership.** The company's push for a new, open identity came with full support from the top. Doyle himself starred in the videos, speaking bluntly to the camera about the brand's shortcomings.

2. **Make a brag sheet.** Domino's still, of course, did a lot of things well. They were groundbreakers when it came to delivery, promising to get a pizza to you in a hurry. Their people were also passionate about food, and they loved pizza. Doyle often stressed what was good about the company, and everyone rallied around fixing what was faltering.

3. **React to feedback intelligently.** Doyle's own response to the feedback from focus groups was telling.

He accepted what the commenters were saying, but he did not allow it to shake his faith in the brand. "You can either use negative comments to get you down," he said, "or you can use them to excite you and energize your process of making a better pizza."

4. **Fake it till you make it.** We'll never know how Domino's people felt about the new, honest approach, but they certainly came back with a swagger. "We're going to do an end-zone dance on this one," said one of their chefs as they zeroed in on a new recipe. From the minute the campaign launched, the brand acted like it had a winner.

5. **Repetition, repetition, repetition.** This one is a little obvious for Domino's, but they stuck to their guns, and as it turned out, they had a pretty good pie. Sales rocketed upward, and the brand recovered.

Awesomeness Will Suggest Itself

Over time, believe it or not, a strong identity and action will also suggest great ideas. By focusing on who you are, you'll start to see opportunities that others won't. The reason for this is that your perspective is its own, and you'll be the only one inspired by it. Once you start to activate your new identity, you will further differentiate. Once you start to get creative, that's when the magic happens.

For example, Domino's eventually used its focus on

transparency to inspire a one-of-a-kind web and mobile app. Like any of its rivals' apps, you can use it to order pizza, but it also has a unique tracking feature. It tells you in the moment what's happening with your pizza, who is making it, and who will be delivering it. It may not be the reason you order pizza from Domino's, but it clues you in to their culture, makes a human connection, and gives you a good idea of when the pies will arrive.

Another example of being inspired by action is Best Buy, which for years was one of the most maligned brands on the planet. The Apple Store ate its lunch on a quality experience, while Amazon turned it into a showroom where people would go to look but not to buy. Many of its brick-and-mortar competitors caved under the pressure from these two dynamics alone.

Best Buy realized, however, that it had one advantage that Amazon did not have: real live human beings with a decent level of knowledge of the products it sold. Buying electronics is one of the more complicated purchase processes most of us encounter. There are so many options, the technology can be confusing, and it's very easy to end up with the wrong thing.

To counter this, Best Buy changed the role of its salespeople. Rather than only trying to drive sales, they were encouraged to become friendly consultants, offering advice and information to help people make the right decision for themselves, not necessarily for the store.

This identity eventually inspired one of the most successful uses of digital technology by any retailer. Best Buy turned all of its friendly salespeople and Geek Squad technicians into @Twelpforce. This was a Twitter handle that was shared by

3,000 Best Buy experts. You could ask any question—even ones about products Best Buy did not sell—and get a knowledgeable reply almost instantly. Over the four years of its existence, @Twelpforce sent out 65,000 helpful tweets—and presumably turned many of the recipients into serious fans of Best Buy.[29]

@Twelpforce is no longer with us, but that's just because the brand realized it wasn't always twelpful to answer questions about complex technologies in 140 characters or less. In a drive to be even better, the brand rolled the service into an online community called Best Buy Unboxed. Today, while the community itself answers many of the questions, helpful Best Buy employees are still there to jump in and answer the toughest ones.

Action suggests action. As you start to live your identity, the direction you need to move to continue strengthening your identity (and its uniqueness) will eventually suggest itself.

Love at Second Sight

You might be wondering at this point, what if I get it wrong? What if my identity actually doesn't work? This has happened, of course, many times. JC Penney famously hired an Apple exec who promptly tried to turn it into more of an exclusive brand. That was a bad strategy for a venerable name in everyman discounting.

Acting with conviction does not mean acting with blinders. One of the great things about digital media is that feedback is nearly instantaneous, and if it is persistently negative, it's time to reevaluate. JC Penney didn't listen when its sales plunged and customers complained, which did serious financial damage to the company.

Fortunately, you get more than one chance. Love at first sight has a mythic quality about it. It makes for a great movie scene, and in truth, it does happen. But pining away for the perfect person turns out to be a bad idea. Researchers have found that searching for that perfect someone who completely matches our needs and desires from the minute we meet often leads to unrealistic expectations and difficulty. In fact, one study showed that only 11 percent of people said their long-term relationships started with love at first sight. It's just not how it works in the long term. Instead, we initially make a good impression, and then the impression is deepened as time goes on.

Points to Remember

- **Ignore first impressions.** The initial reaction to your new identity and action may be muted or even mildly negative. Don't let that discourage you.
- **Pivot if you're making a really bad impression.** There's a difference between people being a little startled by the change and many people actively hating what you're doing. If you're filled with the latter, retool and start again.
- **Figure out what works.** Marketing is an iterative process, where we continually check what we're doing and adjust activities according to what works. Even though you have a strong identity and act with conviction, you

do need to keep your ear to the ground to make sure you shift in the direction your customers are going.

- **Remember, you have more than one chance.** People don't necessarily fall in love at first sight. As they get to know your brand over time, they may grow to like it more and more.

Case Study: Burberry

Let's look at a final example of how to adopt a new identity and carry it through action to success. In 2006, Burberry had long been watching its luxury rivals leap ahead. The brand was in global disarray, with twenty-three licensees around the world making different products at varying price points. It was trying to be all things to all people, which is something no luxury brand (or most brands in general) can afford to be. Sales were sinking and investors were grumbling.

Into the CEO's chair came Angela Ahrendt. At the time, however, she was a curiosity, and the British press being what it is, they made sure that her whole history as a cheerleader from a small town in Indiana was known to everyone. But Ahrendt had a great brag sheet—twenty-five years of experience in the industry with people like Donna Karan—and the confidence to fix what was wrong.

In the fashion business, identity is largely visual, and under Ahrendt's watch, the brand soon coalesced around a simple, nostalgic vision. It reached back 150 years to the first and most iconic Burberry product: the trench coat. Under her leadership, Burberry would revive it, champion it, and hold it up as an icon.

The product itself and its Britishness would serve as a solid point of luxury distinction. Let's see how the brand followed our steps:

1. **Exercise strong leadership.** In an article written for the *Harvard Business Review*,[30] Ahrendt described how she selected a close-knit team dedicated to the concept of the trench. They encountered plenty of resistance and even had to testify before the House of Commons when they decided to invest in their home plant in England and close other offices and facilities in places like Wales. But because they stayed dedicated to an identity inspired by their heritage, they persevered.

2. **Make a brag sheet.** One of the great things for a brand about selecting a nostalgic identity is that you have a built-in brag sheet. The company was founded by a twenty-one-year-old who invented a new kind of fabric, and it had for years stood as an iconic brand. Its coats had been worn by Ernest Shackleton, numerous movie stars, and for years the royal family. The new identity fused the idea of a heritage brand with a young innovator.

3. **React to feedback intelligently.** The luxury business is highly cyclical. During flush times, sales go up, and during downturns in the economy, it suffers. Brands that lack confidence are tempted to stray from their identity, perhaps offering cheaper products or, gasp, discounting. Burberry's position on this is clear. As

Ahrendt wrote: "We've always said we're not immune to the ebb and flow of the macro economy, but that doesn't change our vision. We have absolutely clarity about—and commitment to—our proven strategies, which gives us confidence for the long term."

4. **Fake it till you make it.** You might think that the refocus on a single product would narrow the creative palette of Burberry's designers. After all, prior to the change, some offices were even making kilts and outerwear for dogs. But the strong identity actually unleashed a torrent of creativity at Burberry. Its once staid line of coats was transformed with bright colors and patterns, capes, and shorter coats. On the marketing side, that bled into a new social community, "Art of the Trench," in which photographers compete to post pictures of Burberry customers wearing the coats. It has drawn in millions of the brand's most engaged customers.

Most importantly, the new identity helped the bottom line. From a sagging brand that seemed headed toward a comfortable retirement, Burberry rebounded to double its revenue in five years—all by refocusing on a simple coat and riding its tails wherever they went.

What's Next?

At this point, it might make sense to take a quick look back and consolidate what we've observed so far about attraction. We started out with a bold idea: that brands could use some serious relationship advice. By looking into the psychology behind attraction, we uncovered some simple truths that could help us understand how to navigate a much more personal marketing world.

First, we looked at pickup lines. We saw that they had some value. After all, everyone likes a good joke and a warm smile. But a steady diet of pickup lines does not project confidence or make you attractive, even if all of that communication is on brand. You have to do something deeper.

From there, we outlined three major focus areas to strengthen our brand-esteem. First, we selected an identity, based on a vision of the future or a return to the past. Next, we focused on creating energized differentiation, or how our brand would be unique and different. Finally, we looked at action, and how the simple act of living your identity can get you started and even open up new avenues of creativity for your brand.

At this point, we've found a way to put forth an attractive, confident brand presence. In the next half of the book, we'll look at something different—not attracting customers, but keeping them and making them love you. It's one thing to get a lot of dates, it's quite another to find someone you can spend the rest of your life with. But if we want serious lifetime value from our customers, we're going to have to understand what they truly want from us and how we can deliver it—day after day.

PART 2

RELATIONSHIPS

WE'VE ALL KNOWN PEOPLE WHO DO WELL IN THE BAR scene on a Friday evening, but no one can stand to be around them on Saturday and Sunday. As a brand, you're not looking for a one-time attraction. You're in the relationship business, through and through.

Building good brand relationships is not easy. But just as we've all known a pickup artist, we also know the polar opposite. Some people are simply good at relationships. They not only get married and stay married, but they establish deep connections to friends and relatives. They may be indifferent at attracting partners, but when they do, they know how to keep them.

Some brands also have a knack for connecting and getting people to fall in love with them. Typically, they're the ones that marketers talk about so much that no one wants to hear about them anymore. Of course, that kind of love and loyalty starts with great products, but typically the best brands also present, sell, and communicate in deep and meaningful ways. They connect with us.

This is what the second half of this book is about. It outlines a series of principles and techniques for making people love you long-term. It's about building affinity, encouraging investment, and staying fresh and relevant.

First, though, we have to acknowledge the elephant in the room. *Relationship* is one of the most overused and misused terms in marketing. It's also usually aspirational. We expect some long-term reciprocal interchange with fierce loyalty and extreme advocacy. We think of how grown men will argue endlessly (and occasionally exchange punches) over whether Chevy or Ford makes the best pickup truck. Or we think of those people who drink a six pack of Diet Coke a day and can't live without it.

Let's not get ahead of ourselves. Just as we've seen that not all brands can be attractive in the same way, not all of them can have the same kinds of relationships. And that's fine—actually, more than fine. Maybe you won't have people writing fawning reviews about your products on Amazon, but nearly every brand can build better and more lasting connections, at least with some part of its audience.

In the following chapters, we'll shed light on the question of what people really want from us and how we can deliver it. We'll start with the most basic of all questions: how do you extend a simple product relationship into something more real? We'll see that one of the most important things is to find points of intersection and establish leadership in an area your audience cares about.

We'll also look at what kind of responses people want from you and how brands can become more empathetic—in small ways and large. Finally, we'll look at reciprocity and investment, and understand the seemingly contradictory fact that brands that ask more of their customers often get more in return.

Through it all, we'll come to understand what successful couples around the world often learn: while being on the dating market seems like a lot of fun, it's actually difficult and stressful. It's tough and scary to forge a new identity and put it out there. It's much easier and more fun to get in the slipstream of your customers' passions and build something they'll appreciate and maybe even grow to love.

CHAPTER 7

THERE'S SOMETHING TO BEING A CLINGER

Key Takeaway

PROXIMITY IS A HUGE PREDICTOR OF WHETHER OR NOT people will fall in love with each other and brands. Most great brands find ways to be present in their customers' lives beyond simply providing a product or service.

Introduction

Among many of its other important contributions to our world, the film *Wedding Crashers* introduced the term *Stage 5 clinger*. The phrase was spoken by Jeremy (Vince Vaughn) about Claire (Rachel McAdams), whom he fears is becoming attached to him too fast. In the years since the movie's release, the term has come to denote a borderline stalker, someone who is so obsessed with another person that it becomes creepy.

Interestingly enough, however, that's not the lesson the movie teaches. Jeremy actually starts out the movie as a committed single guy, trying to rack up as many flings as possible. Over the course of the story, he falls in love with the obsessive Claire, and the two get married. It turns out there's something to being a clinger.

Psychologists have long known that proximity is one of the more reliable predictors of relationship success. And by this, I don't mean to say that long-distance relationships can't work. But anyone in a workplace has seen relationships, even unlikely ones, blossom when people are thrown together for extended periods of time. It also turns out that college students in Dorm A are much more likely to date people from that building than those in Dorm B. This fact is so widespread that psychologists have dubbed it the *Proximity Principle* or the *Mere-Exposure Effect*.[31]

The *Proximity Principle* has big implications for brands today. While we've always been able to reach out and advertise, we can now be much more present than ever before. We can respond quickly to complaints and praise; we can even target our customers accurately with ads and content whenever we like. We can create forums or even products that allow them to interact with us on a daily basis. That has created an entirely new set of expectations from customers—both positive and negative.

Just as there's a fine line between clinging and stalking, you can go overboard or under the radar with this. Some brands annoy us by littering our feeds with too many communications. They use data to target us in ways that seem invasive. Then again, others are too cold. They only reach out when they have a new product to sell, or they respond to legitimate complaints with canned messages and corporate-speak. They don't seem to sympathize with us or understand our problems.

In this chapter, we'll dig into this challenge and find ways to make the balance work. We'll look at why it's important to listen hard, speak when spoken to, and manage our communications without overwhelming anyone.

Nuts for Airlines

One of the most unlikely success stories in digital media is the airline industry. That's because while most of us like to travel, almost all of us hate to fly. Lines are long, security is annoying, and even ordinary things seem to cost extra.

Not surprisingly, airlines were initially reluctant to go on social media. They knew that when they opened up, their feeds would soon be filled with people trashing them for everything from stale peanuts to weather delays. (In point of fact, airlines get no breaks: they are one of the few businesses that regularly get blamed for the weather.)

Of course, they were right. People vented their frustrations. Airline brands scrambled to contain the damage, and it wasn't fun. Soon, however, the smarter carriers realized something important. Rather than sticking people with bad service, they could now quickly identify and resolve complaints. If some customer's dear cat Fluffy got inadvertently routed to Albuquerque, they could make sure she had water and treats.

The very best at navigating the new landscape has to be

Southwest Airlines. When we hear its outreach efforts discussed, it's often characterized as a social media strategy, but in reality, we could call it a clinger strategy. It's about being there 24/7. If you want a Southwest brand experience, you get one. The airline has a popular blog and website, and a presence in nearly every channel. It responds within an hour to every post about it, and its answers are individualized and signed with the first name of the employee who is responding. They even come with the occasional typo.

Southwest reaches out almost daily with new content for its surprisingly popular *Nuts About Southwest* blog. To accomplish this remarkable output, it calls on all employees and customers to contribute stories, which include everything from the history of the airline to tearjerkers about flying with sick children. It's hard to imagine that people could emote with a business in an industry that everyone dislikes, but they do.

All of this is backed by what the company calls a "listening center" that monitors any mention of its brand and uses the information to respond, develop services, and figure out what its customers want. And it seems to work. Unlike almost every other airline brand, Southwest has gotten the message that not even the rich and famous like to pay extra to check a bag.[32]

As we'll see, all of these activities—responding, listening, and creating fresh avenues of communication—are important building blocks in making relationships work, including those between brands and customers.

Brand Proximity

From a psychological perspective, the *Mere-Exposure Effect* is not rocket science. Human beings are wired to like things that are familiar to them. We may say we're up for adventure, but most of us are secretly boring and love routines. We have a particular chair at home that we sit in every day. We like our comfy blankets and our favorite pair of slippers. Changes in a morning routine are usually met with irrational frustration.

It makes sense that the more we spend time with someone, the more likely we are to build a relationship, romantic or otherwise. But here's the catch: with more people online looking to build relationships, we tend to be physically disconnected. This has some interesting implications for brands. Since most of our outreach—and frankly, our entire clinger strategy—is digital, will we be able to truly build a relationship? Or do we need to be physically present?

Plenty of research has gone into trying to prove that social media and other online outlets do not produce deep friendships. (There's a certain grumpy-old-man aspect to research about social lives on the Internet, probably because grumpy old men are paying for it.) And of course no one would deny that there is something inherently shallow in our connections to many of our online friends. They're often not so much friends as people with whom we once upon a time shared a high school.

But if, in general, we don't have tight bonds with our social friends, that doesn't mean we can't form meaningful connections digitally. In fact, we do so all the time. As of 2013, a shocking one-third of all US marriages were the result of online dating.[33] (You may want to read that twice). Psychologists have also studied video gamers, who have a tendency to form close bonds with other players halfway around the world. By playing together regularly and chatting about their lives, they form entirely virtual relationships. Initially, you might think these would be second-rate friendships, but in fact, gamers tend to rate their online friendships as deeper and more meaningful than their "real" ones.[34] In other words, proximity is a construct that we can use not merely in the physical world but in the digital one as well.[35]

For brands, this is good news. Even though they tend to occupy a narrower band of interaction with people and don't share a full range of human emotions, brands can be a focused, positive presence in people's lives, especially if they find a way to become part of those lives. Brands now have a channel to work with and an opportunity to figure out a way to cling but not stalk. To do this, they have two options: reactive or proactive. Let's look at these in turn.

Reactive Contact

This is how a brand reacts when people reach out. Sometimes a customer may give a positive *attaboy*. (It does happen.) More often, however, when customers reach out, they have an agenda. They have a complaint or a question, a product review, or a nit to pick. Some brands might think they don't need to respond to every little nitpicker, but here's the problem: people expect them to.

Let's be brutally honest for a moment. People nowadays have very high expectations of brands and absolutely no filter if things don't go the way they want. The Internet can be a deeply uncivil place at the best of times, but when it comes to brands, the four-letter words tend to fly fast. If people are upset, they get on Amazon or a brand's own social feeds and let the world know exactly how they feel about any given situation.

When this happens, we have to jump on it. Southwest's one-hour response time to complaints is no accident. Increased brand proximity has made customers very impatient to hear back. In fact, 72 percent of people expect brands to snap to in an hour or less if they complain on social media. We'll dig into this topic a little more deeply in a moment.[36]

Proactive Contact

The other side of the coin is proactive contact. This occurs any time a brand reaches out to a customer on its own initiative. It includes everything from content marketing and product announcements to highly targeted ads. It's the Southwest Airlines blog or its tearjerking charity stories on Facebook.

Overall, this kind of content needs to build on your brand's identity and position it as a leader. As we'll see, the success of proactive contact depends on finding the key intersection points where you can provide a valuable service but seamlessly sell at the same time.

Intersection Pointing

For some brands, intersection points are dead simple. An athletic company provides training tips and workout tutorials. A fabric company brings in an expert fashion designer or a crafty home sewer with a big social media following. It's more difficult if you're a toothpaste or a cereal brand. But let's see how we can do it.

We can try with cereal. We'll imagine you're the brand manager of a popular brand called Oat Crunchies. You have a tremendous interest in rolling oats to the point that your wife could practically write a book on the subject. However, you've also learned from experience that almost no one shares this passion of yours.

Next, go a little deeper in your thinking about your product. While most eat it in a bowl with a spoon, a few do include it in trail mix. Thinking it through, you realize it's unlikely you have a real shot at becoming a leader in the cooking or outdoor space. Time to do some research.

You need to know what people who buy your cereal regularly have in common. So you bring a group of them into a room. You set up some refreshments made with Oat Crunchies, put on some music, and encourage them to mill around. In the beginning, your little customer meet market produces nothing but a general discussion of your brand (or at least the category in which your brand plays). But soon the conversation wanders. One only has so much patience for a discussion about breakfast cereal. Participants start talking about convenience and getting out of the house quickly. You discover common threads: busy lives, laziness, or the fact that the only way to get their kids to eat is with an iPad streaming Elmo videos. Soon, you start to uncover the orthogonal topics that matter to people who are loyal to your brand.

You can also do this with data. Tools for figuring out orthogonal interests are robust and growing. Amazon Retail Analytics or a set of Twitter searches, for example, can provide insights into the lifestyle and content choices of people who buy or engage with your product or category. Oat Crunchies eaters may over-index on *Sesame Street* or enjoy knitting. You never know.

This kind of analysis leads to action in the real world. For example, it has drawn energy drinks like Rockstar to sponsor professional video-gaming events (eSports). You might not think that a drink has much to do with video gaming, but it turns out that pro video-gamers require intense concentration and eSports are serious, demanding endeavors for those who play them. Many find that high-caffeine drinks give them an edge. That has led to an intersection point where the brand has built affinity.

Finding intersection points takes an investment, but it is critical to setting your brand up for a successful relationship— one that can truly blossom long-term. This is an area worth spending time on to be sure that you find those rich areas of common interest.

Once you've identified the topics of interest that people care about most, your next step is to figure out how it can build a meaningful presence in the discussion over the long haul. For example, if you're managing a beer brand, you might discover that your beverage's target audience over-indexes on tailgating.

Great, but a few grilling tips aren't going to be enough. Instead, you need to dig a little deeper and find a way to add some utility or value to the conversation. Here are some steps for success:

1. **Acknowledge what you want to sell.** If you're trying to build or maintain a relationship, mistrust matters. In the brand space, people are going to cheat on you with other brands a lot more than that, but you still have to be real about why you are getting into their lives. You're selling stuff. It's okay. People get that. Embrace it. Too often brands are apologetic about the fact that they're in the selling business. Brands have a limited amount of time to make a good impression, so be honest and put the product front and center.

2. **Identify an interest intersection point.** Whenever we meet someone, we need to find those things we have in common. Brands have intersection points with people, and we merely have to uncover them.

3. **Sell *and* serve.** Southwest does this by creating content, of course, but they also listen heavily to understand what people want from them. In business terms, what does your brand's audience need? What do they ask for? Not just with your brand, but in the world? What can be done to drive that forward? How can your product be the hero?

Case Study: Sharpie

To see how this can work, let's look at a recent successful example. In 2012, Sharpie was a dominant brand, but it wasn't creating excitement among young people. You wouldn't really expect it to—Sharpie is essentially a suite of office products, and I think none of us needs a reminder of how Millennials feel about offices. (Let's face it, we're right.) Nonetheless, the brand looked at orthogonal interests of this audience and discovered it had an intersection point: young people value creativity and like to be original. It says something about who they are.

And so, the brand decided to support youth art through its products. It built a forum for sharing art, went into social media, and enlisted young artists to create content. It hired noted illustrators to create tutorials on how to get more out of a pen, held contests with real prizes, and soon had a thriving community of young people interested in and excited about the brand.

So let's go through the same steps to see how Sharpie serves and sells:

1. **Acknowledge what you want to sell.** Sharpie is always present in its content. Although there is not a pen in every drawing, almost every piece of content shows what you can do with one. It's actually very important for this brand in particular to keep the product forward. It exists in a crowded category where almost everyone buys by making a snap decision in-aisle. Making sure the brand is mentally present is incredibly important. So Sharpie makes itself visible and available.

2. **Identify an interest intersection point**. Art and creativity may not seem natural for Sharpie; the number of people who wake up in the morning and shout, "Yay, I get to mark up a financial report today!" is admittedly small. Yet the brand found an intersection point with young people and pushed itself into that area by offering something in return—sometimes a prize, but more importantly the fame of appearing in the Sharpie community. The brand has continued to find further points of intersection. Recently, for example, it realized that its most passionate creative types enjoy a good jolt of espresso to get the ideas flowing, so it put forward a dedicated effort around drawing on Starbucks cups.

3. **Sell *and* serve.** Sharpie makes itself useful in two ways. First, it inspires people to find creativity everywhere. Second, it provides a forum where people can express themselves, get props, and enjoy a creatively elevated life. But the interesting part about it is that to take part in this burgeoning Sharpie community, people must also buy the product. The selling is a built-in extension of the service. The more you get into the community Sharpie has built, the more of its products you'll buy.

With this strategic approach in place, Sharpie saw a 5 percent increase in product sales over a two-year period. While that may not seem like a lot, this is a massive brand with more than 50 percent penetration. Growing sales in a mature category is tough, but by finding a way to be present and then selling and serving, Sharpie managed to do just that.

Happy and Unhappy Customers

Proactive contact is the fun stuff, the sexy stuff. It's about finding creative ways to cozy up to your hopefully happy customers. So let's finish up with a slightly drier and more boring question: how do we react correctly when people reach out to us for the other reasons—when they want to praise or complain?

Essentially, the rules are very similar to the rules we've all learned in life. Let's start with praise. Today, if someone leaps onto a Crayon's social feed and says, "I really love my new purple Crayon box," most brands would reply according to brand positioning: "Glad to see you're feeling the purpletastic love."

Sounds good right? Well, not so much. Imagine if someone at a dinner party praised your meatloaf and you replied, "I'm glad you're digging my personal recipe for beef and porktastic love." At that point, your spouse would be entirely in the right to give you a sharp kick under the table. The basic rules of politeness for praise are simple and eternal. Acknowledge the compliment, say thank you, and move on. Or modestly deflect the comment. "Thank you! I'm not much of a cook; I just got the recipe from Jamie Oliver. Do you want it?" That's it.

Now, let's look at negative comments. As we've seen, every brand steps in it occasionally, and we've covered that deeply in Chapter 4. But making a misstep is not the only problem you might have. Your customers might not be able to figure out how to put together the lawn sprinkler, or their kids might have discovered that the washable markers permanently etch Mom's marble countertop.

Of course, if you can, you try to jump in and provide a solution to the problem. Otherwise, you have to do what everyone should (but often doesn't) do in a relationship when a partner is upset: be present and listen, be responsive and helpful, and use those insights to get better.

Be Present and Listen

Let's imagine your partner comes home from work and says, "My boss was such a jerk today. I just hate when he criticizes me in front of the rest of the team." One of your options is to say, "Then get a new job." We hardly need research to tell us (though we have it) that this is not going to work. At this moment, she isn't necessarily looking for career advice, she just wants to vent. She's had a bad day, she's on an emotional ride, and she will feel a thousand times better if you'd just sit there, nod your head, and say, "Yes, I understand." Your job is to first to listen and acknowledge what has been said.

To see how this can work in a business context, imagine you have been waiting three hours for a late plane and you get on social media to complain that all the restaurants are too expensive. In scenario one, the airline replies, "We're sorry you are experiencing a delay. Here's a voucher for $25 off on your next flight." That's not bad, but it doesn't really show they were listening or cared. In scenario two, the airline replies. "Oh, that sounds like you're really hungry. Here's a $7 voucher you can use right now at any of the restaurants in the terminal." Being present means knowing what's been said, acknowledging the feeling, and doing something that makes sense in the context of the moment. It works in personal relationships, and it does a lot for brands.

For another example, let's say that you've ordered a new printer and it doesn't work. In scenario one, the company says, "We're so sorry to hear that. We're sending a new one." That's a reasonable response, but it's hardly one that makes anyone happy. It's a little like when a child breaks a toy, and Dad says, "Stop crying, we'll get you a new one." It may be just my observation, but it seems that when confronted with that solution, the child invariably does not stop crying, but cries more; he or she was holding out hope that instead of being callously indifferent to her distress, the all-knowing Dad would be able to fix the thing. She does not want a different toy on some vague day to be determined later; she wants some form of immediate resolution—mainly the same broken toy not to be broken right now. She wants Dad to understand why she's crying and acknowledge that it's okay.

Likewise, the customer doesn't want another printer; that's a hassle. She wanted the printer she has to work the first time. Or she wanted customer service to tell her that there is a magic button on the bottom of the printer that causes it to instantly heal itself. Barring that, she expects a little human sympathy and to find out that you've thought through her concerns. She wants a response like, "Oh no, that's got to be frustrating. Hopefully you didn't have anything pressing to print. We'll rush another one to you by tomorrow." In this way, the brand acknowledges what the person is feeling and responds in a human way. Don't think this makes a difference? Give it a try.

Be Responsive and Help-Oriented

The second rule is to always help if you can. Rather than dismissing his child's concerns by offering to buy another one, the dad above might have applied his brain to setting things right. I've often seen around families that Scotch tape works much better to mend broken toys—and hearts—than a credit card.

Likewise, a speedy offer to exchange or refund a product is nowhere near as good as trying to think through the problem and come up with a solution. A printer brand that was thinking on its feet might partner with a retailer like Best Buy to quickly exchange products.

Become an Insight Collector

Listening is magical not only for crafting a good response but also for keeping your pulse on what consumers are thinking about. There are millions of mini–focus groups going on about matters that you, your business, and your brand care about. It's a good idea to be out there hearing what's being said. A brand doesn't need to act on everything, but there is a tremendous opportunity to learn about and anticipate trends in the market. You'd be surprised by what you can learn, anticipate, innovate around, and avoid—showcasing how in touch you are.

Consistent Contact

While being there and showing some empathy is important, you can also smother people with too much contact. So how much is too much?

For an answer to this, we can turn back to our Internet stars. From hearing about them, you might think being a big personal brand like Hannah Hart, PewDiePie, or Vlogbrothers is a cushy job. You just be yourself, talk into a camera, and *voilà*—a million dollars magically appears in your bank account each year. Unfortunately, that breezy description does not seem to be true. Videos are hard. They need to be staged, shot, reshot, and edited. Scripts have to be written, concepts developed, and ideas constantly generated. PewDiePie's profanity-filled video-game sessions may seem completely off-the-cuff, but he reportedly works ten-hour days. Hannah Hart travels around quite a bit, but everywhere she goes, she finds a kitchen in which to drink a new booze and destroy a new recipe. What seems fun and easy is actually a grind.

And yet, combing through all the advice given by Internet stars, only two pieces are consistent. The first, predictably, is to be yourself. The second is to be consistent about publication. If you want an audience, you need to feed it new content regularly. You can't slack, you can't let up, and you can't take a break.

In sum, brands can't look at a relationship as a series of campaigns or a process driven by a product launch cycle. We have to decide on an ongoing plan of outreach that puts us in proximity to our customers when it makes sense. For some, that may be daily, for others a few times a year. But whatever that rhythm is, we have to find it and stick to it.

What's Next?

Being a clinger is a good thing if we manage it in a helpful, productive way. Like Claire in *Wedding Crashers,* brands have to put in some hard work. The simple fact is that no one gets to be a great brand without being present in people's lives. For reactive content, we have to respond to the marketplace with helpful and timely ideas and intervention. For proactive content, we need to find places where we can serve our audience and at the same time sell to them. Only by approaching proximity in this way will we find a welcome place in our customer's lives.

CHAPTER 8

OPPOSITES DON'T ATTRACT

Key Takeaway

IF YOU WANT TO BUILD A RELATIONSHIP WITH PEOPLE, YOU have to resonate with them in a positive way by creating strong bonds through shared interests. The easiest way to do this is by infusing your points of intersection with deep levels of topical knowledge to become a leader. Luckily, that doesn't mean you have to build deep expertise in all topics. It merely means that you show that you understand your customers' concerns by reflecting their interests through deep savvy with a focused set of relevant matters.

Introduction

Now that we've identified some important points of intersection, you're probably thinking, "Great, we'll just step forward into the conversation with our unique identity and be done with it." That's the easy route, but it's not necessarily going to get you very far.

Like it or not, brands are held to a higher standard when it comes to relationships. We each may have dozens of friends we care about, but we only care for a small number of brands. My personal number is five, and I'm a marketer who's into that kind of thing. Civilians probably like even fewer brands, if any at all.

When we do care about a brand, it's because it offers more than a product; it offers something of value, something we can identify with. It may be exceptional experiences like Apple or thoughtful marketing like Yeti's that speaks to something deep within us.

In this short chapter, we're going to expand on the ideas of the last. We'll see why brands can seriously benefit by not merely sharing interests but by championing them. Leadership for marketers is a tricky but not an impossible task. As we'll see, you don't need to build a wealth of knowledge across all of your intersection points. You merely have to dive deep into an aspect of them that resonates deeply and builds an authentic connection to those you are trying to reach.

Innovation Leads the Charge

To see how a brand can provide leadership at an intersection point, let's start with one of the best. Virgin is a company that supports an entrepreneurship movement. It fosters it, practices it, and sponsors it. The company's identity is not wrapped up in a specific product (because it has so many) but rather in an on-going charge to reinvent, reimagine, and help people experience things in new ways. That drive has led it to change how people bank, travel, listen to music, work out, and much more. In other words, it has a point of view that everything should be rethought and redone with an entrepreneurial mindset—everything. Of course, Richard Branson is the ultimate embodiment of this idea.

If you look at the company's digital properties, you'll find a focus on encouraging people to dream big. Virgin devotes an entire section of its top-level website navigation to entrepreneurship. Click on it, and you'll find yourself immersed in a world where everyone is trying to build a better mousetrap. The emphasis is on youth (from looking at the site, you might get the impression that leaving college early is the best move you could make), and the focus on youthful entrepreneurs gets even more specific—nurturing those who have a great idea but need to get up the courage to take the plunge.

This approach serves only a small part of Virgin's audience, perhaps, but it's emblematic of the business as a whole. Virgin builds a deep affinity with its entire customer base. The company's approach seems to work for a number of reasons:

- **It displays deep knowledge.** If you want to know how to start a business, any business, Virgin has content to help you succeed. The company has dug into the personality traits of successful entrepreneurs, asked what they like for breakfast, and championed hundreds who have succeeded—and then broken the information down into simple pieces that anyone can understand.
- **It demonstrates authority.** Virgin does this, of course,

by opening new businesses. Whatever you say about Virgin, it is a place where lots of pioneering ventures are started and make their way into the world by standout entrepreneurs and intra-prenuers. So the company has the authority to show you how to get it done. Virgin lives that greater calling by helping to instill a sense of confidence and courage in those who are hesitant to even get started. To Virgin, it certainly doesn't matter if 90 percent of startups fail.[37] It's the process and the courage to reinvent that it is energized by.

- **It illustrates everything with stories.** Stories sell, and the entrepreneurship section of the Virgin site is filled with them. The company celebrates wins (and even attempts) by others, not just its own.

Of course, you could easily say that not everyone has a Richard Branson, who is actually the star of Virgin's show. Fair enough—there is only one. But he's successful (and successful at attracting avid fans) for a reason. Let's dig in and find out why.

Going Deep

The Virgin playbook is really simple: take what you do well and champion it in others. This should give us a pretty good idea of how we can start to work on a relationship with our customers. Much like Virgin does, we have to tap into who our customers are and want to be—even it's only for a brief moment at a time. To do this, we have get out of the shallow end of the pool and build our knowledge around shared interests.

This is a point made perhaps most saliently by Chris Malone and Susan T. Fiske in their book *The Human Brand*. They highlighted a large body of research (much of it by Fiske herself) that shows how we are innately attracted to competence. We like brands, the authors argued, if they seem to know what they're doing.

To take one example from the personal-brand world, we could look at Michelle Phan. Perhaps you don't know her, but that's probably because you're not a female adolescent and aren't trying to look as beautiful as you can. Phan does makeup, and even though she's not a trained beautician (or perhaps because), she is astonishingly good. Want to look like a Goth princess? She'll show you how. Bleach blond? No problem. Redheaded skater chick? Grab your hair dye. And she'll go even further than that. She can help you channel your inner zombie, purr with cat eyes, and do things that, quite frankly, are utterly baffling to someone like me, who has never opened mascara before. She has a nice personality, of course, but her entire brand rests on her ability to lead and empower her followers to look more fetching on Friday night.

Brands should expand their depth of competence around the points of interest they share with their customers. Some, like Ben and Jerry's, have gone all-in for social justice. Patagonia loves the environment and supports a range of programs from growing organic to making its supply chain more transparent. Yeti has championed the fading ranks of serious outdoorsmen.

Nearly every brand has someplace it can dig in. Of course, this brings up a problem. Typically, most brands sit in rather broad categories: tools, cleaning products, health food. If you make health food, you're going to have a big problem. If you Google "gluten-free," you get 113,000,000 search results. To say it's a crowded category where it's difficult to stand out is the very definition of an understatement. So let's see what you can do.

Narrowing Your Focus

For some brands, the only way to gain separation from the crowd and become relationship material is to go deep but narrow. After all, competence and leadership come from knowing something really well, not having good general knowledge. A soda brand may comment on pop culture, but it's not going to be as informed about it as *TMZ* or *Entertainment Weekly*. Those guys have celebs on the brain 24/7.

Instead, you can focus on a smaller subset of your category, a place where you can have a unique perspective and truly lead. If you're a sports-clothing company not named Nike or Under Armour, it may be better to start focusing on certain sports— even odd ones—rather than do everything so-so.

You might think a narrow focus destines you to a small audience, but that's usually not the case. To see why, let's imagine you are a brand that believes in preserving the environment. People only have so much time for the environment (and less, frankly, than it deserves). And while it's odd to say it, you're going to be "competing" for mind-share not merely with other brands but also with the Sierra Club. If you do so in a bland, on-brand way, it's going to be extremely difficult to add value to the conversation. Crickets are, of course, a nice thing to have in the environment, but when they're the response to your marketing, that's not a good thing.

If, however, you make yourself a champion of endangered box turtles that are losing their habitat thanks to encroaching civilization, that will be much more interesting to people. Cynically speaking, box turtles are cute and interesting creatures, and they make for great cartoons. More importantly, you'll be able to research the problem better than most people. If you partner with conservationists, you could use your megaphone to promote new, interesting content. It will be visually rich, emotionally poignant, and above all focused. And you'll have a chance to make a real difference, without breaking your budget. That is leadership and working for change.

In many cases, leadership is not about encapsulating every value that your customers have. It's about positioning in a way that encapsulates the values of your brand and adds something to the conversation. If you can do something they care about in a small way, they'll understand that you share their overall values.

For a completely different example, we can look at how you can build on what people already like about you. Like many businesspeople, I am grateful for Uber—and not merely because they've solved the whole taxis-are-a-total-pain issue, although that's nice. If that's all Uber did, I would certainly not sneeze at them. But I'd probably be just as loyal and engaged with Lyft.

But Uber does more than simply take me from point A to point B. It addresses larger personal-transportation issues as well. For example, last year Uber sent me an email a few days before Halloween. It was about what Uber called "the two a.m. problem." In the US cities, bars close at two in the morning and typically disgorge thousands of people who need a ride. The email explained that Halloween is an unusually difficult time for this. Cars are scarce, surge pricing goes into effect, and you end up waiting a long time and spending a small fortune for a ride. Uber suggested two ways out. First, it shared its data on Halloween and showed the hours you'd want to avoid using the service. In addition, it suggested using its new Uberpool service, where you share rides with others. It led the way to a more rational and considerate use of transportation. People like me are fans.

Communicating Like a Leader

Great leaders need to be able to communicate. It's one thing to take a bold stance and lead in a particular direction, but we also have to be able to communicate our affinity to our audience.

In a 2005 study, a team of researchers compared the speeches of presidents perceived as great speakers, such as Lincoln, Reagan, and Roosevelt, with those perceived as fairly dreadful ones, like Herbert Hoover.[38] They isolated a number of traits of great communicators, the most interesting of which were metaphor, contrasts, and stories. Each of these is primarily a way to create a communication shortcut that grabs a person's imagination. As we think about the speed and volume of brand messages that an individual person receives, this is getting to be more important than ever. Any way that we can simplify and focus ourselves will enable us to communicate better, faster, and with greater clarity.

Metaphor

We're going to bury the competition, let's take the bull by the horns, the buck stops here—all of these are familiar expressions that instantly convey a wide sense of emotion and meaning. The perfect metaphor takes very complex concepts and simplifies them so they resonate instantly with people.

Use of Contrasts

"Ask not what your country can do for you, but what you can do for your country." Contrasts have a deep emotional and connective effect. Leadership brands tend to be good at framing things in contrast to other things—and in particular as different from their competitors. Steve Jobs famously urged us to "Think different," putting Apple in its own category. Less effectively, but in the same vein, Google said "Don't be evil," subtly suggesting that everyone else was.

Transformative Storytelling

Often when politicians talk, they reference their personal or their constituents' stories. For example, if an economist laid out why a certain student-loan bill would benefit society, you might nod politely. A good politician might take a different tack and talk about a person she met on the campaign trail who worked at a supermarket and dreamed of sending her kids to college.

In fact, researchers who have studied storytelling have come up with the theory of a *transportational story*.[39] This particular kind of story takes our attention off the present and transports us to a different world. Such stories, they found, are much more persuasive than simple facts.

Here's an example: Penzeys Spices is a beloved brand among a certain segment of serious home cooks, even though it has largely ignored every bit of advice given to traditional brands. It has never posted to social media, its website is mediocre, and its CEO is highly opinionated. If you want to know how strange it really is, it sells primarily through a paper catalogue. Nonetheless, it has grown steadily over the past twenty years and has a vociferous fan base.[40]

Much of Penzeys' success is the result of what it features in its catalogues. Unlike most cooking brands, it has not embraced the celebrity chef. Instead, it seeks out ordinary customers with interesting stories, often with a social-responsibility message. People read the stories (which often have nothing to do with food) and then see how the person uses the product (often with only moderate skill). These transportational stories seem to drive the brand forward. At last count, its catalogue has 600,000 recipients.

Naming Your Tribe

Naturally, if you're a leader, it helps to define your followers. For a simple example, a few years ago, retailer TJ Maxx was looking for a way to pump up enthusiasm among its customers. People liked its fashion-for-less approach, but it still wasn't something they could wear with pride. In a great move, the brand decided to build affinity among them by giving them a name: Maxxinistas, a clever jab at fashionistas (who presumably looked down on the brand). It helped set TJ Maxx apart and became a symbol of pride for those who embrace the retailer's low-cost fashion-emulation model.

You find this more commonly in musical brands. KISS refers to its fans as an army. Lady Gaga has her Little Monsters and Katy Perry her Katy Cats. But brands can do this as well. In addition to TJ Maxx, Finnish housewares company Fiskars has its Fiskateers and Urban Decay its UDers.

Such names are a great step in identifying and rewarding a loyal following. This may be a small step, but if you want to build relationships, giving people a rallying point and making them feel like they are a part of something bigger is a good place to start.

Finding the Right Megaphone

Finally, we should make sure we're communicating in the right place. For example, imagine for a moment that you run an organization dedicated to raising money for disaster relief. Your marketing director bursts into the room one day and says, "I've just uncovered a brilliant opportunity. We just learned that 10 percent of our biggest donors now have Snapchat accounts. We should go on Snapchat."

You think about it for a moment and say, "But we're trying

to raise money. It doesn't help us to be on a platform where our message disappears before people can do anything with it."

This is an extreme example of finding the right megaphone for your message, which is the final part of the equation for building an audience with affinity. The right megaphone means that you're not only hitting your target audience but doing so in the proper context. Brands today have a range of ways to reach out and get their message across, but the industry has largely fallen into a practice of channel-specific strategies. This is a lot like our old way of looking at media. You find your audience and then you target it with the message you want. If you want the young male demo, you have one set of places to meet them; if you are targeting mothers with small children, you have another.

You want to select a medium or platform for your message, but you also want to make sure it doesn't create dissonance. Facebook and Instagram are fairly broad mediums for sharing a wide range of things. Targeting your desired audience on those social platforms is always okay, but almost every other platform is more restrictive and requires some thought.

As the technology advances, we'll need to choose our megaphones in ever more thoughtful ways to stay in tune with (and continued to be welcomed by) our audience. As a side note, this is yet another reason why picking an intersection point of shared passion and adding value to the conversation will be even more important moving forward.

What's Next?

To build affinity with customers, we simply need to focus. We have to find those narrow bands where we can really strike a chord with people. We have to take a leadership role and then tell the right stories in the right places. Doing all of these things will draw like-minded people to our brands and will set us up for a long-term relationship that goes well beyond a simple transaction.[41]

CHAPTER 9

DAILY ATTRACTION: DEVELOPING AN EMPATHETIC PERSONALITY

Key Takeaway

WHEN BUILDING A RELATIONSHIP, BRANDS MUST DEEPEN their strong identities (who they are) and personalities (the way they express their identity) so that they can respond empathetically and with situational awareness in real time. A little upfront work makes spontaneous engagement much easier.

Introduction

For over half a century, good brands have prided themselves on their personalities. At best, they were the life of the party, cracking jokes, inspiring trust, and generally good to be around—for thirty seconds at a time. Once upon a time, you could build a really strong connection that way. In addition to making people laugh or cry, you could set the terms of the conversation, and your audience really had no choice but to go along with you. Some found your stance attractive and worthy of attention. Those people became loyal fans.

But as digital media evolved, the conversation began to flow both ways, and brands found their personality and narrative increasingly difficult to define and control. The central challenge that most brands face is to preserve a great personality but deepen it and use it in a much more empathetic way. The Marlboro man may have just needed a face (and later a lung transplant) to get his message across. His successors need to think on their feet too. Their personalities need to become more fluid and situationally aware, so that they can build a real relationship with customers in a digital age.

The Human Connection

To see how a responsive and empathetic personality works in real life, let's imagine you're a single woman with a mother who likes to play matchmaker. She calls you up and tells you about a spectacular guy she's found for you. We'll call him Frank. She tells you he's an entrepreneur: dynamic, funny, successful, and oh-so-good-looking. Of course, Mom's a little nearsighted and not exactly Yenta of the Year, but when you do your own Facebook stalking, you realize she's on point. Frank gets your number, and after a brief chat you book an evening together and expect sparks to fly.

Frank shows up and nails the initial stages. He arrives with a single red rose. He has a good plan for the evening: a casual dinner and a stop at an improv club. He also doesn't make a big deal when you mention that you want to split the tab (nor does he seem overly relieved).

He also turns out to be a nice guy. He has a ready stream of funny stories, has traveled a lot, and knows his way around a wine list. But as the evening progresses, something about him starts to bother you. He doesn't really pay attention to what you're saying. He talks about what he wants—about his interests. And above all, about his startup. Whenever you add a point or tell a personal story, he doesn't seem to hear you. He has no curiosity about you. He doesn't care what you think, and he's not interested in what you say. He always brings the conversation back to his favorite topics. Before the date is halfway through, you want to be at home with a door between you and the possibility of seeing him again.

His problem? He didn't react or flow. He didn't listen to you. He didn't respond to anything you said. He had a good personality on the surface but no empathy or interest in what you were adding to the conversation. While his approach may work great while talking to investors in his startup—who are interested in listening, not sharing—ultimately it failed in making a connection or building a relationship with you.

Personality vs. Empathy

One of the more fascinating studies on the subject of personality and empathy was released in 2016 by, of all places, dating site Match.com. Essentially, it sought to answer a burning question: what makes someone successful at hookups? In investigating which approaches work in scoring a fling and which don't, the researchers found that people who were more successful in seduction shared a common trait: they used emojis a lot. It turns out that a smiling, laughing face or even a suggestive eggplant (did the world really need an emoji for eggplant?) tends to elicit a better response, irrespective of other factors.[42]

Psychologists explain this with a concept called *emotional contagion*. While it sounds rather ominous, it's actually a big part of how we forge friendships and romantic relationships. It turns out that people who are close to one another often catch their emotions, much as you might catch a cold. This is actually fairly logical if you think about it. If your spouse is stressed, you become stressed. If your best friend is overjoyed at winning the lottery, you feel happy too (and expect a free lunch or two). Emotional contagion is a major way that we connect.[43]

When it comes to the Match.com example, we all know that emails and texts don't generally convey much emotion—and when they do, it may be the wrong emotion. Many an office blowup has been caused by someone reading the tone of a hastily sent message. Emojis shortcut that. By definition, they put the feelings in that the text leaves out. They can show you're listening and responding with appropriate emotion. As a result, you can build emotional contagion, i.e. connection, much faster.

The lesson here is not necessarily that brands need to start using emojis (though it is interesting how few do). Instead, it speaks to the fact that we need to develop our ability to listen and understand what people are feeling. As much as possible, our personality cannot be static anymore. It needs to understand and respond to the context in which our customers are happy, sad, frustrated, or elated.

As you might expect, most brands don't really do this. They are more like Frank, employing what we called earlier a pickup-line strategy—using personality as a filter for content that never seems aware of any interaction that has come before or after. Frank has an outwardly good personality, but his emotional radar is poor. Similarly, most brands have pretty good personalities, but they may lack the ability to respond like a human at any point, let alone in real time. They tend to be the same, no matter what. Let's dig in and find out why this was once a great all-up strategy but has now become a first step to build on.

The Foundations of Personality

To start, we need to understand the foundation concept of brand personality that once built success. In doing so, we can take a page from a well-received book on the topic, Margaret Mark and Carol Pearson's *The Hero and the Outlaw: Building Extraordinary Brands Through the Power of Archetypes*. The authors sought to understand brand personalities through archetypes, a concept borrowed from psychologist Carl Jung. For Jung, archetypes represented structures in the collective unconscious. In an oversimplified way, you can think of them as ideas that we all carry around in our brains without explicitly being aware of them. There is an archetype for *mother*, for example, and one for *heroes* or *patriarchs*. In fact, Jungian psychologists have never quite nailed down how many there are, or even if there is a limit to the number that exist.

Mark and Pearson were more specific. They proposed

twelve brand archetypes, with names like *Innocent* and *Sage*.[44] Each of them, the authors said, had six dimensions: desire, goal, fear, strategy, trap, and gift. The idea was that great brands could use these as templates and guideposts to developing great brand personalities.

To see how this works, we can look at two iconic brands: Nike and Jack Daniels. Their particular archetypes are best explained by Douglas Holt and Douglas Cameron in their book *Cultural Strategy: Using Innovative Ideologies to Build Breakthrough Brands.*

Let's start with Jack. In the 1950s, Jack Daniels was one of a number of small distilleries producing Tennessee whiskey. These were largely indistinguishable from one another, and none had much of a following. At the time, Tennessee whiskey didn't fit into the fabric of American life— quite literally. Fifties culture was largely conformist. It was the era of the company man, the tract home, and the gray flannel suit. The signature social event was the cocktail party, where people ate canapés and drank martinis until one of them put on a lamp shade.

Jack Daniels did not fit into this picture at all. For starters, Tennessee whiskey is not a cocktail beverage. You can make a handful of drinks with it, but compared with brandy or gin, it doesn't mingle. It's a liquid loner. In the 1950s, it was also a 90-proof kick in the face. You didn't sip Jack politely, you shot it down because you were a tough SOB and could handle the hard stuff.

The Jack Daniels brand came to terms with this in a unique way. It recognized that Tennessee whiskey wasn't the only thing that didn't fit into 1950s culture. A lot of people also felt left out of it. They didn't want to attend polite cocktail parties. They didn't want to fit in. They wanted to be rebels. This was also the era of beatniks, street gangs, and motorcycle clubs. Jack Daniels decided to embrace this undercurrent of society. Led by a local advertising agency, it began to develop a personality infused with individualism and masculinity. It became the antiestablishment drink, the Harley Davidson of the bar. It was for loners and outdoor types who didn't go with the flow.

Backed up by big ad buys, this personality worked brilliantly. Within a decade, JD had become a worldwide icon. Today, it still touts itself as the brand of freedom-seekers and individualists—and it remains a top seller. In archetypal terms, Jack Daniels fits neatly into the "outlaw" category.

The Outlaw	
Desire	Freedom from social restraint
Goal	Break the rules, beat back authority
Fear	Going too far, being seen as weak or conformist
Strategy	Advocate for the little man, rebels, and those who break with conventions
Trap	Going too far, hurting people
Gift	Strength, integrity, know-how

Jack Daniels, of course, didn't consciously set out to use an archetype (though a Jungian would argue it did so unconsciously anyway), but this one does fit its personality to a T. And in an age of print and TV, that built a worldwide brand. The more people became exposed to the drink, the more of them drank it. Its outlaw personality worked.

Our second example, Nike, shows how a good personality could once intersect with—and even drive—a cultural movement. It's hard to imagine, but in the mid-1980s, Nike primarily served athletes, who wore the shoes for sports, not style. The company's sales were steady but small, and the brand was considered aloof and factual.

At the time, people were beginning to become excited about exercise and body image. The upstart Reebok had capitalized on this trend by focusing on the aerobics market. It produced lines of athletic shoes that were not merely athletic but also looked good on those who wore them. As a result, Reebok's sales soared while Nike looked on.

At that point, Nike called in Dan Weiden of Weiden + Kennedy. Impressed by the company's positive attitude, he supposedly said, "You Nike guys, you just do it." Whether this story is true or not, "Just Do It" became one of the most famous slogans in advertising history. It positioned Nike in archetypal terms as a hero brand, encouraging and enabling extreme performance. As a hero brand, Nike has a different set of attributes from Jack Daniels.

The Hero	
Desire	To prove one's worth through courageous and difficult action
Goal	Exert mastery in a way that improves the world
Fear	Weakness, vulnerability, "wimping out"
Strategy	Become as strong, competent, and powerful as you are capable of being
Trap	Arrogance, developing a need for there always to be an enemy
Gift	Competence and courage

The brand conveyed this personality with a wide-ranging series of campaigns that convinced Americans that the path to better fitness and bodies lay through the hard and sometimes tedious work of training. It also enlisted master athletes to reinforce the message. If a pair of Nikes and hard work could propel Michael Jordan to great heights, it could certainly improve performance for the average Joe.

Partly thanks to Nike, the idea of "gain through pain" gathered enormous cultural significance, even though there is little scientific evidence for it and a growing body against. Ask most people what it takes to be healthy, and they assume it involves intense exercise. If you're not working hard, sweating, and suffering, you won't be fit. Over time, this notion has spawned ever more punishing forms of training, like Beach Body and CrossFit. In this way, Nike has helped create a "truth" that is firmly embedded as common sense in our culture today.

The Dimensions of Interaction

As the digital age has progressed, Nike has not rested on this strong archetypal personality. While it still projects its hero image through advertising, it has also experimented with and invested in a range of technology platforms that support its customers. Its (former) Fuelband product offering was one example of the many ways it has provided support, encouragement, competition, community, and information. It has fully embraced that hero personality but discovered new ways to respond and react to customer needs in a digital age.

While personality alone had extraordinary power in an era of thirty-second spots, it has to be reactive and empathetic—to have multiple dimensions—to succeed today. If you've ever speed-dated, you know that anyone can be pretty much anyone for thirty seconds at a time. In a digital and social media age that carries with it increasing depth and frequency of interaction, we have to expand and understand our brand's personality at a level that is so much deeper.

At this point, you're probably wondering, "Wait a minute, how can I maintain brand identity in such an always-on, engagement-rich environment?" Here's a dirty secret: it's not as engagement-rich as it seems. In fact, people have less time for us than ever. Moreover, while brands have to respond in human ways, they don't have to be human. They exist in a much narrower range of interaction. Nobody wants to talk about the weather with a brand. No one wants to take one out for pizza. People don't expect brands to cry on their shoulder, or vice versa. (Okay, in times of sorrow, we do occasionally seek out a tub of Ben and Jerry's, but that's not the same thing.)

There are only a few dimensions we really ever need to worry about, the most important of which are escape, information, tribe, and apology. People will look to you from time to time for a brief moment of escape (likely an intriguing ad). They are going to want to know things about your products. If you're lucky, like Harley Davidson or Red Bull, you'll occasionally be a part of their tribal identity. And sometimes, unfortunately, you're going to have to say you're sorry. In all of those contexts, both in planned ads and in-the-moment responses, you'll need to be able to respond empathetically with your personality. Let's look at each of these dimensions in a little more detail.

Escape

Escape is a fairly straightforward offering. Whenever we can take people away from their present lives for fifteen seconds or five minutes and provide them with a brief emotional hit (laughter, tears, and everything in between), we start to build a relationship.

If you're looking for a stellar example from the content world, Buzzfeed has thrived by providing brief moments of escape. That's what it does. For example, it has a whole series of amusing videos in which Americans try out popular junk food from other countries for the first time. Imagine the look on their faces as they snack on dried squid balls, roast chicken–flavored chips, and fiery dried chickpeas. This is not content of earth-shattering importance, but it does provide escape.

Most brands have similar opportunities. Escape is, after all, what good traditional thirty-second spots offered. Of course, the content must resonate with your brand's personality, its identity, and the interest intersection points we uncovered in the previous chapters. And it must do so in a much deeper way than most brands have traditionally done.

We have numerous examples, but the outdoor space provides some of the best. Brands like Yeti and Patagonia, for example, highlight the lives of outstanding outdoorsmen (and women), often in touching, emotional, and/or aspirational ways.

Yeti in particular has struck a chord. While the brand sits in a largely undifferentiated space, it has staked out a bold claim with six-minute videos about hardcore outdoorsmen. Its "My Old Man" series, for instance, displays an old-school masculinity that sometimes borders on the antisocial. One of its subjects, for example, takes his young son on a dangerous boar hunt and arms him with a bow and arrow. But the glimpse into an extreme world provides an authentic form of escape that deeply resonates with the brand's fans.

Information

Any time a brand offers advice or recipes or creates a how-to video, it is providing information. Done right, this content reflects a nuanced understanding of the brand's customers. For example, Kraft Foods largely makes convenience foods, and as might be expected, it has a site that offers recipes on how to use its products. A stunning 1,182 of them have the word *easy* in their title.[45] These recipes are geared not merely to making good food but also to making sure you don't have to spend much time doing it. In other words, Kraft does not try to compete directly with the enormous number of recipes crowding the web; it doubles down on the specific intersection points of quick, easy, and delicious family meals.

Tribal

At the deepest level, you have the opportunity to be a highly authentic cultural force. One way to do this is to champion micro-segments. The Yeti videos we've discussed do this by highlighting extreme outdoorsmen who have often highly specialized pursuits. But pretty much any brand can at least try for tribal.

Toyota likes to be playful and fun in its communications, often portraying its customers in less serious ways than its competitors. A few years ago, the brand urged families to embrace the minivan with Toyota Swagger videos, in which an extremely ordinary-looking family rapped about life in the suburbs. People tend to find the videos either the worst or the best thing they've ever seen. The music is absolutely horrible, but with 13 million views, the brand clearly struck a chord among those who are—usually not by choice—forced to drive the least sexy type of automobile on the planet.

Apology

Up until now, we've been discussing the need to be strong in your identity—but every brand will also screw up sometimes. It may be your fault, or it may simply be that you were doing something that no one seemed to mind until it suddenly seemed terrible.

Moments to say "I'm sorry" can range in severity, but they have one common thread: they never come on schedule. Most complaints are quite predictable, though, and you can plan for different scenarios and develop a general playbook for success. You'll have product issues, employees losing it on Facebook, poorly treated customers, or people who misunderstood what your product does. You should have thought-out responses for everything from modest flubs to major ones. While you can never avoid being surprised, you can be ready when it happens—dodging a one-day wait (ahem, United).

Building a Responsive Personality

Most brands will see their efforts to deepen their personalities manifest primarily in the digital and social space. This includes everything from answering the occasional tweet to responding to complaints on Amazon. While each of these personality dimensions can foster in-depth discussions, digital also enables you to enroll people and engage with your customers every day—building unparalleled familiarity with your brand. To do this, you'll need to equip yourself (or a team) with the tools to listen and provide feedback that responds in an empathetic way to what people are saying.

To see how this can work, let's zero in on a brand that has had, on the whole, an up-and-down ride over the years: Whole Foods. Launched in 1980, it has grown largely with the public's interest in moving away from a highly processed diet to one that emphasizes fresh food and a wider variety of ingredients. Today, it is nearly ubiquitous in large cities and affluent areas.

But it also faces the same problems as any company that deals in healthy or natural foods. The category is highly fad-driven, with huge swings in public opinion and information over time. Nutritional science, like psychology, is complicated, and what seems to be the case from one study is often disproved by the next. As a result, a modest and vaguely conclusive research paper about a particular ingredient can set off a major trend, even though the science later questions itself. What's more, it can change according to geography. The Northeast may want to be vegan, while the South insists that good health is synonymous with buttermilk biscuits.

Companies like Whole Foods have to navigate this landscape and be aware of what people want on a local level. They need to adjust their personalities to reflect their humanity and respond to local interests. And so, Whole Foods recently reinvented itself on a much smaller model. Individual store management in every community now has a heavy say in brand communications. Each store has its own social media stream, manned by its own people. They offer unique deals, product trials, philanthropic opportunities, and more. Of course, they all understand the brand's personality, but they have the freedom to put a deeper local stamp on it. They can read the mood of their customers and change the discussion (even offerings) according to customer needs. This puts each store at the center of consumers' relationship with food, tapping into their interests in a way that is perfectly mindful of their desires.

What's Next?

In this chapter, we've explored the concept of brand personality in a free-flowing digital context. Essentially, we've seen how personality is a full expression of your identity. It's not merely who you are but how you interact with people and respond to their desires. While traditionally we could simply project personality, now it has become a more fluid construct, one that we need to dig into and practice to get right. Luckily, we have focused on a starting set of dimensions in which it has to operate. That simplifies our task and opens up new avenues for creative thinking.

CHAPTER 10

NICE GUYS DON'T REALLY FINISH LAST

Key Takeaway

NICE GUYS DON'T REALLY FINISH LAST. NOR DO NICE brands. The best brands are not only good to their customers, but they also ask for a small investment in return. It need not be much, but it drives a mutual relationship that can be strong or subtle, depending on the brand's approach.

Introduction

No marketing book would be complete without a full chapter devoted to some form of advocacy. That said, I cringe when I hear people say that we need to turn our customers into advocates. Such a statement implies that we can create walking ads for our brands, passionately spreading the word.

Let's get real for a moment. People aren't going to put their personal reputation (not least their reputation for sanity) on the line to yell about how much they love your window cleaner. They only have a limited amount of time in a day, and they touch a vast number of brands. We have to come to grips with the fact that a brand like Disney will have a different definition of advocacy from most brands. One may be strong and passionate, the other muted but appreciative.

As Thomas Gensmeyer—founder of Blue State Digital and one of the masterminds behind Barack Obama's digital campaign—has often said, advocacy does not need not be very passionate. All it means is that a person does something on your behalf. In a political context, Gensmeyer would happily take a donation or a lawn sign. He does not need you to fork over your life savings. Disney, of course, gets massive advocacy. It can expect its fans to spend a small fortune to wear an authentic Star Wars stormtrooper costume to Comic-Con. Most brands, however, don't need customers to tattoo a logo on their arms or shave it into their heads. They merely need them to invest in some small way in the relationship.

In this chapter, we'll see that a brand strategy of mutual investment is based on sound science, and there are many examples of it in the real world. While you can build a good brand by being nice, reciprocal relationships are much stronger. You need to make yours a two-way street by mastering the art of mutual brand and customer investment.

The Paradox of Being Nice

Do nice guys really finish last? Sometimes it seems like it. After all, we all know those jerks who have terrific significant others and treat them like toads. They're always demanding things and being selfish. They may even get away with it. But while this undoubtedly works for some people in some situations, being nice turns out to be a better strategy overall.

Studying "nice guys" is a tough topic, because *nice* is one of those words with a lot of different meanings. When psychologists define it as being altruistic and giving to others, nice is an attractive trait to have.[46] For example, an oft-cited study had women look at two dating profiles of men, both of which featured the same photo; the profiles, however, were different. One of them, nicknamed "nice Todd," had subtle cues that he was a sweetheart, while other had cues that indicated he was a jerk. "Nice Todd" crushed the competition in that one.[47]

However, *nice* gets slightly more complex when it comes to relationship dynamics. That's because once you're in a relationship, being nice doesn't merely mean that you're sympathetic, empathetic, or altruistic. It more often means doing something you'd rather not for your partner's benefit—prioritizing your partner's career over your own, perhaps, or giving her a night out, or letting her sleep in while you take the kids to a soccer tournament at eight in the morning. As people, we tend to term these things as *nice*, but psychologists typically prefer the term *investment*.

Investment is where it gets interesting. You might think that when one person invests in the relationship, the other feels more obligated to it. But people aren't logical that way. If you invest in a relationship by getting out of bed early and making eggs Benedict, you are the one who invariably feels better and more committed. The effect on your partner can be positive, neutral, or even negative. Often, people reply to unexpected kindnesses with a quick, "Okay, so what did you do?" This invariable sets off a fight.

The explanation usually given for these divergent reactions is that the doer of kindnesses has invested in the relationship. He or she now has sunk costs into it and has a stronger incentive to make it succeed.[48] "What has he done for me lately?" is a question that's worth asking if you're wondering whether he's committed to the relationship.

Investment is also the reason why being nice can go wrong. If you're weak-willed and always giving in, that's not going to work. In the first place, it won't make you attractive as a potential partner (you'll be seen as a pushover). And if your partner doesn't invest too by making compromises, his or her commitment to the relationship will be weak. Nice guys don't necessarily finish last, but they do if they're with someone who doesn't give back.

So nice guys and girls rejoice! You don't have to be a jerk to win over the object of your desire. You merely have to make sure they're playing nice too.

The Invested Consumer

This concept has big implications for brands. Right now, most brands make additional investments in their customers beyond simply providing a product or service. We offer help, deals, support, and free content. You might fool yourself into thinking that you can build a breakout brand by being great to your customers and winning their loyalty through gifts. But you actually build such brands by providing ways for customers to invest in you as well.

Obviously, whenever someone purchases a product, they are investing in the relationship. But not all purchases are equal. If you can, think of two things you've bought recently. They should be around the same cost. Now let's imagine one of them you simply bought on the spur of the moment because you had to have it. That's probably not something that stays in your mind. Now think of a product that you've seriously researched, like a connected speaker, a piece of furniture, or a car. If you have spent a lot of time looking before the purchase, you are much more likely to mention it in conversation with friends and talk about its virtues, independent of anything the brand has done. The simple act of choosing Samsung or Apple often causes people to become loud advocates of their choice, even though the company's products are functionally similar.

In addition, as we've seen in today's much more personalized landscape, interactions and relationships between brands and customers have gone far beyond this. We can invest not merely with purchasing behavior but also with the effort we take to learn a new technology. For example, almost anyone who has put in the effort to learn and use a Fitbit will become attached to it. They've invested in it by working out, sharing their data, and tracking their fitness. As a result, some will, without any further prodding from the brand, discuss its advantages with friends. And while they may know little to nothing about a

Microsoft Band or Jawbone device, they will flatly state that their Fitbit is better.

On the flipside, one-sided investments (in which the brand does all the work) *don't* build loyalty. Brands that offer discounts, coupons, or loyalty cards tend to be weaker than those that demand everyone pay the same price all the time. Columbia, a clothing company that is very quick with offers, does not command anywhere near the price premium of some of its rivals, like The North Face, even though the quality of its products is probably good enough for most people. And strong brands like Apple or Kitchenaid do not, as a matter of policy, ever discount.

The important thing is to get your customers to invest by not merely purchasing your product but devoting some amount of time, money, or effort as well. If this sounds counterintuitive, let's look at some ways you can succeed with it.

Ask for Love (Not Like)

Nearly every pizza parlor and nail salon wants you to like them on Facebook and follow them on Twitter. This is not the worst tactic. It's a small, yard-sign investment that we're looking for. The main problem with this is a technical one. Facebook doesn't want brands to have free advertising on the platform, and so it suppresses brand content. That's why you should aim a little higher. Asking for a review on Yelp or Amazon is a small step every brand can take. It results in a modest investment that can help people stay in a relationship with you.

Sell a Membership

An increasing number of retailers these days are offering memberships, sometimes at a substantial cost. In many cases, buying one may seem like a purely rational decision. We invest in a Costco membership not because we like Costco very much but because we expect a return on that investment in terms of savings over traditional stores.

But investment is not always so straightforward or mercantile. An excellent recent example is Amazon Prime, which charges $100 per year for free two-day shipping and other goodies. With this, you don't necessarily get a price break, and you still have to wait two days. But there is something about the act of buying into the service that makes us much more likely to use it.

Other retailers have found even more clever ways to exploit the concept of investment. REI sells a lifetime membership for $20, which is actually a share of a cooperative. Every year, each member of the co-op receives a rebate on purchases based on how much the entire collective has bought. The rate of the rebate changes based on the actions of the entire cooperative. If co-op members spend, say, $100 million in the course of a year, it might be 10 percent. If they spend $200 million, it might be 15 percent. In this way, the co-op creates a cyclical sunk cost that recurs every year—and pretty good loyalty.

At the highest end, you might look at American Express. Its $400/year platinum card is a big investment, but it unlocks far more than that in value for the customer, including front-of-the-line privileges at airports, elite status with hotel chains, credits for fees charged by airlines, and so on. That creates a strong bond and sense of mutual responsibility. Want to know how strong that sense is? I'm a member, and I feel obligated to mention it here.

Build a System

Platforms are extremely powerful but available only to the lucky few. They involve anything that allows you to invest periodically in the relationship. The concept is obvious to anyone who's watched Apple, whose mobile devices have die-hard fans even though they are functionally similar to rivals. It's also a fact that Apple fans are often awed by the introduction of features that have long been available on other platforms. Part of the reason is that fans have invested heavily in music and apps in the Apple Store and are loathe to switch—and the more invested they are, they louder they become.

Indirect Investment

There are also non-technological ways to build investment in a product or product line—in particular by getting customers to invest in learning something that requires your products. An example here might be King Arthur Flour, which teaches legions of home bakers how to create artisan loaves—and not incidentally induces them to buy a lot of specialized gear to do so. The more King Arthur gets people educationally invested in baking, the more likely those people are to buy the company's products.

Conversely, it's great if you can involve people as educators. Software companies, for example, often create MVP programs, where they declare customers experts in the use of their products. That requires a certification class and is an investment that naturally makes these users core evangelists for the brands.

Community

Communities are a great way to get people to invest. Any time you're building something where your customers can offer advice, answer questions, or contribute content, you've giving them the ability to feel better about themselves, improve their self-esteem, and also invest in your process. Companies like Cross-Fit build strong micro-communities (some might call them "cults") where members get together to work out and bond. As a result, people are quite loyal to the brand and find it difficult to leave.

A similar sense of community is fostered, as we saw in the last chapter, by Whole Foods, which brings people in a neighborhood together not merely to shop but also for online and in-store events. This allows people to invest in the brand and brings them closer to it.

Beta Testing

A quite different opportunity extends to brands that create digital products. Software and gaming companies, for example, offer beta programs that essentially offer players or users an advanced look at the product. (Google's Glass Explorer program was probably the best known and most notorious of these.) In exchange, customers try it out, find bugs, and offer feedback.

Needless to say, such programs are great at getting people to invest in a product. They may be getting an advance look, but they're also trying it out and working for the brand, usually for free. As a result, they become invested in the product and will feel loyalty and pride when the item is finally released. They'll also brag endlessly to their friends about their membership in the program—which is a great form of advocacy.

This also works for non-technology brands and products. Giving highly loyal or active consumers early access to new products or even the opportunity to give feedback on creative (packaging, videos, etc.) can enroll them into the brand early and create feelings of investment.

Wrapping Up

Obviously, these are only some examples of how brands can create opportunities for consumer investment. But it's easy to see that the more you can make people invest themselves in your brand and its success, the stronger they'll advocate. Harsh fights erupt between advocates of Ford and Chevy or iOS and Android because people do have a substantial investment in them. Those in a beloved community will naturally feel more loyal to the brand that has fostered it. This is not because of any rational calculus but because they have sunk costs and have feelings of obligation for all the brand has given them.

It's important that brands find small but meaningful ways in which customers can contribute to the company's success. Give people a stake in the outcome, and you'll find they actually care about it.

What's Next?

It may seem bizarre or even risky to demand that your customers do things for you. But human nature dictates that that this is one of the strongest ways to create a deeper connection between two things. As I said, it's not that nice guys finish last. You can be as nice as you like, but you should ask for something in return. It may be small, but it has to be something—and the more you can foster investment, the stronger your brand will be.

THE JOURNEY TO SIMPLIFICATION

If you're like me, every morning starts with a glance at a feed filled with links to articles. Each one contains a handful of statistics, usually with warnings, predictions, and recommendations on what companies should be doing. In addition to that, you probably spend much of the day in meetings and presentations where yet more data is presented. You try to keep on top of emerging platforms and gathering trends, even though there are so many of them. Frankly, if you let this all get to you, it might make you feel like you're under about ten feet of water and you forgot your scuba gear.

Typically, you have two ways to attack the situation. You can read as much as you can, you can listen to podcasts, and you can end up spending all of your time trying to be as informed as possible. That's the hard way, and it's very much the path our industry tends to follow. Everything, we are told, is unique. We live in a brave new world in which behavior is radically changing. We have to treat everything as different; we have to master each new thing individually. That's why, for instance, you often find someone asking for a Snapchat strategy or a digital strategy or a millennial strategy.

The second and easier way is to come up with a framework that simplifies and categorizes all of the input you're getting. Rather than trying to master the ins and outs of different developments, you develop a framework or a handy set of boxes into which everything can fall. Instead of dealing with many unfamiliar objects, you have a fast way to associate them with familiar things. At best, such a framework allows you to see things in a simple, human way that is easily understandable to anyone.

Brand attraction can provide this framework. It doesn't answer every marketing question you'll encounter. Obviously you do need to look at Gen Y differently from Gen X. And if your strategy leads you to Snapchat, you'd better understand exactly how people are using it. But attraction provides a metaphor that simplifies how we look at the modern marketing landscape. People are accessing media and spending time in different ways, but they've not changed their aspirations—and especially not their desire to make meaningful connections with each other and to a much lesser but real degree with brands.

Rather than seeing fourteen different social platforms, you can view everything as a landscape in which you try to attract people and build a lasting relationship. This is something we all intuitively get. We've all been that kid desperately in love with someone and afraid to talk to him or her. We've all had that relationship where we were overly committed, and our partner liked someone else more. We've all learned to put ourselves out there in a club or at a party and been shot down. This is something we get.

When we use brand attraction as a framework, we can much more easily understand what we're trying to achieve in today's bewildering landscape. It's not about mobile or digital. It's not about social or even CRM. It's about finding the right place to drop that initial pickup line. It's about having a strong identity, projecting confidence, being there for people, and listening to what they have to say. And then it's about doing things that deepen the relationship and create mutual investment. In this way, brand attraction can simplify a world that seems hopelessly complex and put it into actionable terms.

As I said in the beginning of this book, my parents know almost nothing about the field I work in—at least not in the true technical sense. They have little idea about the mechanics of determining the proper media mix or facilitating a programmatic buy. But they can easily understand the basics when I use relationship-speak. Likewise, it's much easier for me to design a strategy and present it to a CFO or CEO when I'm not trying to deal with all the detail of today's marketing machinery. If we get too caught up in the mechanics, it gets difficult to see the big picture.

The second big advantage of brand attraction is one that you might not imagine at first: it helps us make better use of data. We often celebrate the arrival of Big Data and believe that we're doing things rationally and scientifically, rather than "by our guts." Instead of making decisions based on intuition, we can make them based on the solid insight provided by numbers.

In truth, it's hard to make sense of so much data—we may

even have too much. So why not embrace attraction as our first reality check, our first filter? It can prompt the questions we need to ask and allow us to better interpret the outcome. After all, it's always people who have to look at the numbers and determine what they mean. Something like investment or empathy could become a collection point for data and provide a lens through which we understand the importance of a campaign or our efforts.

But above all, brand attraction brings an element of simplicity to the conversation. In truth, marketing today is no harder or more complicated than it ever was. Ever since the first store opened or the first exchange of goods was made, we've always had a simple desire to sell products to people who want them and develop a trusted relationship over time. Originally that was a personal relationship, but as brands have come into being, the same basic truths hold. We merely have to translate the simple concepts we know from our lives into the world of our work. And if we can keep our heads level and follow the rules we all instinctively know, we can be as successful in marketing as we hopefully are in our personal lives.

∞

ENDNOTES

1   Dillon Baker, "The State of Messaging Apps, in 5 Charts," *Contently*, June 2015, https://contently.com/strategist/2015/06/30/the-state-of-messaging-apps-in-5-charts/.

2   Recommendations for these lengths vary from study to study. The numbers here are merely given as an example. They come from Kevan Lee, "Infographic: The Optimal Length for Every Social Media Post and More," *BufferSocial*, October 2014, https://blog.bufferapp.com/optimal-length-social-media.

3   "Hannah Hart," *Wikipedia*, accessed March 17, 2016, https://en.wikipedia.org/wiki/Hannah_Hart.

4   Twitter's search for its own identity is widely reported and ongoing. See "Twitter," *Wikipedia*, accessed March 17, 2016, https://en.wikipedia.org/wiki/Twitter.

5   Ipsos, "Social Influence: Marketing's New Frontier," 2014, accessed March 3, 2016, http://www.slide-share.net/victori98pt/social-influence-marketings-ne w-frontier-by-ipsos-mediact.

6   These brand Twitter screw-ups are well catalogued, but for one source see: Kim Bahsin, "13 Epic Twitter Fails by Big Brands," *Business Insider*, February 2012, http://www.businessinsider.com/13-epic-twitter-fails-by-bi g-brands-2012-2?op=1.

7   Associated Press, "Expert: Malfunction Caused Outage," *ESPN*, March 21, 2013, http://espn.go.com/nfl/story/_/ id/9082144/relay-device-malfunction-caused-super-bow l-xlvii-power-outage-according-expert.

8   For details on the story, see: Angela Watercutter, "How Oreo Won the Marketing Super Bowl With a Timely Blackout Ad on Twitter," *Wired*. February 2013, http:// www.wired.com/2013/02/oreo-twitter-super-bowl/.

9   Norman P. Li, J. Michael Bailey, Douglas T. Kenrick, and Joan A. W. Linsenmeier, "The Necessities and Luxuries of Mate Preferences: Testing the Tradeoffs," *Journal of Personality and Social Psychology* 82, no. 6 (June 2002), 947–955.

10 Kleinke, Meeker, and Staneski, "Preference for Opening Lines: Comparing Ratings by Men and Women," *Sex Roles*, vol. 15, nos. 11/12 (1986).

11 Kleinke, Meeker, and Staneski, "Preference for Opening Lines." Please note, the research findings here are general. Current research into pickup lines has started to segment by personality type and found, for example, that for some people, cheesy pickup lines actually work.

12 Stephanie Strom, "Sales Slide for Mondelez, Maker of Sweets," *The New York Times*, February 2015, http://www.nytimes.com/2015/02/12/business/mondelez-q4-earnings-drop-as-commodity-prices-rise.html?_r=0.

13 "VlogBrothers," *Wikipedia*, accessed March 17, 2016, https://en.wikipedia.org/wiki/VlogBrothers.

14 It's worth pointing out that good looks and high confidence and self-esteem are correlated. The better-looking you are, the more likely you are to be confident. It's possible, however, to have only one of the two, and if anyone ever gives you a choice, choose confidence.

15 H. Krasnova, H. Wenninger, T. Widjaja, and P. Buxmann, "Envy on Facebook: A Hidden Threat to Users' Life Satisfaction?" Paper presented at the 11th International Conference on Wirtschaftsinformatik (WI), Leipzig, Germany, 2013, accessed April 6, 2016, http://www.ara.cat/2013/01/28/855594433.pdf?hash=b775840d43f9f93b7a9031449f809c388f342291.

16 Todd Wasserman, "Red Cross Does PR Disaster Recovery on Rogue Tweet," *Mashable*, February 16, 2011, http://

mashable.com/2011/02/16/red-cross-tweet/#74IlW.
mZ5SqB.

17 Dean Praetorius, "The Red Cross' Rogue Tweet: #gettng-slizzerd on Dogfish Head's Midas Touch," *The Huffington Post*, February 16, 2011, http://www.huffingtonpost.com/2011/02/16/red-cross-rogue-tweet_n_824114.html.

18 This is a very well-researched topic, with many studies confirming the ideas in the following section. Rather than footnoting every sentence, I'll advise you to see "Physical Attractiveness," *Wikipedia*, https://en.wikipedia.org/wiki/Physical_attractiveness.

19 Fiona Macrae, "Skin Deep: Beautiful Faces Have Miss Average Proportions," *Daily Mail*, December 2009, http://www.dailymail.co.uk/sciencetech/article-1236636/Skin-deep-Beautiful-faces-Miss-Average-proportions.html.

20 Paul Eastwick and Lucy Hunt, "So You're Not Desirable ..." *New York Times*, May 2014, http://www.nytimes.com/2014/05/18/opinion/sunday/so-youre-not-desirable.html?smid=pl-share&_r=0.

21 Blatt's "The Rock Band Project" makes for fascinating reading. You can find it at http://www.therockbandproject.com/.

22 Ruth Blatt, "9 Ways to Increase Your Charisma," *Psychology Today*, September 2013, https://www.psychologytoday.

com/blog/the-rock-band-project/201309/9-ways-increas
e-your-charisma.

23 Bruce Temkin, "Which Consumers Give The Most
   Feedback?" Customer Experience Matters, September 13,
   2011, https://experiencematters.wordpress.com/2011/09
   /13/which-consumers-share-the-most-feedback/.

24 Source: Facebook, data retrieved 3/26/2016.

25 Association for Psychological Research, "Grin and Bear It!
   Smiling Facilitates Stress Recovery," retrieved 3/26/2016,
   http://www.psychologicalscience.org/index.php/news/re-
   leases/smiling-facilitates-stress-recovery.html.

26 A good summary of research can be found in Amanda
   McCorquodale, "8 'Fake It 'Til You Make It' Strategies
   Backed by Science," *Mental Floss*, retrieved 3/26/2016,
   http://mentalfloss.com/article/74310/8-fake-it-til-you-ma
   ke-it-strategies-backed-science.

27 For sources for the story, among others see Sam Oches,
   "The Many Acts of Dominos Pizza," *QSR*, August 2010,
   https://www.qsrmagazine.com/menu-innovations/
   many-acts-domino-s-pizza.

28 Domino's Pizza, *The Dominos Pizza Turnaround* (video),
   retrieved   3/26/2016,   https://www.youtube.com/
   watch?v=AH5R56jILag.

29 Matt Newell, "Social Media Case Study—Best Buy's Twelpforce," *Lab Store* (blog), July 2010, http://www.newretailblog.com/social-media-case-study-best-buys-twelpforce/.

30 Angela Ahrendt, "Burberry's CEO on Turning an Aging British Icon into a Global Luxury Brand," *Harvard Business Review*, January/February 2013, https://hbr.org/2013/01/burberrys-ceo-on-turning-an-aging-british-icon-into-a-global-luxury-brand.

31 For a summary of key research, see "Mere-Exposure Effect," *Wikipedia*, https://en.wikipedia.org/wiki/Mere-exposure_effect.

32 Vishal Mehra, "An Exclusive Look Inside the Southwest Airlines Listening Center," *SimpliFlying*, May 2015, http://simpliflying.com/2015/inside-southwest-airlines-listening-center/.

33 AFP Relaxnews, "One-Third of Married Couples in U.S. Meet Online: Study," *New York Daily* News, June 4, 2013, http://www.nydailynews.com/life-style/one-third-us-marriages-start-online-dating-study-article-1.1362743.

34 Y. Amichai-Hamburger, M. Kingsbury, and B. H. Schneider, "Friendship: An Old Concept with a New Meaning?" *Computers in Human Behavior* 29 (2012): 33-39.

35 Christian Martyn Jones, Laura Scholes, Daniel Johnson, and Michelle Colder Carras, "Gaming Well: Links between Videogames and Flourishing Mental Health," *Frontiers in Psychology* 5 (March 2014): 260, http://www.researchgate. net/publication/261764637_Gaming_well_Links_be- tween_videogames_and_flourishing_mental_health

36 Amy Gesenhues, "Study: 72% of Consumers Expect Brands to Respond Within an Hour to Complaints Posted on Twitter," *Marketing Land*, October 2013, http:// marketingland.com/study-72-of-consumers-expect-br ands-to-respond-within-an-hour-to-complaints-poste d-on-twitter-63496.

37 Neil Patel, "90% of Startups Fail: Here's What You Need to Know About the 10%." *Fortune*, January 16, 2015, http://www.forbes.com/sites/neilpa- tel/2015/01/16/90-of-startups-will-fail-heres-what -you-need-to-know-about-the-10/#65f6dd4555e1

38 Mio, Riggio, et. al., "Presidential Leadership and Charisma: The Effects of Metaphor," *The Leadership Quarterly* (2005).

39 Melanie C. Green and Timothy C. Brock, "The Role of Transportation in the Persuasiveness of Public Narratives," *Journal of Personality and Social Psychology* 79, no. 5 (2000): 701–721, http://www.communicationcache.com/ uploads/1/0/8/8/10887248/the_role_of_transporta- tion_in_the_persuasiveness_of_public_narratives.pdf.

40 The liberal political stance of its CEO also generates a good deal of hate too.

41 Among others, see C. J. Lutz-Zois, A. C. Bradley, J. L. Mihalik, and E. R. Moorman-Eavers, "Perceived Similarity and Relationship Success among Dating Couples: An Idiographic Approach," *Journal of Social and Personal Relationships* 23 (2006): 865–880.

42 Laura Stampler, "People Who Use Emojis Have More Sex," *Time*, February 4, 2015, http://time.com/3694763/match-com-dating-survey-emoji-sex/.

43 Sigal Barsdale, "Faster Than a Speeding Text: 'Emotional Contagion' at Work," *Psychology Today*, October 15, 2014, https://www.psychologytoday.com/blog/the-science-work/201410/faster-speeding-text-emotional-contagion-work.

44 For what it's worth, there is no finite number of actual Jungian archetypes, nor do I believe that Mark and Pearson's list should be considered definitive.

45 Source: www.kraftrecipes.com. Retrieved 6/14/2016.

46 P. Barclay, "Altruism as a Courtship Display: Some Effects of Third-Party Generosity on Audience Perceptions," *British Journal of Psychology* 101, no. 1 (2010): 123–135.

47 E. S. Herold and R. R. Milhausen, "Dating Preferences of University Women: An Analysis of the Nice Guy Stereotype," *Journal of Sex and Marital Therapy* 25, no. 4 (1999): 333–343.

48 Jeremy Nicholson, "Make Them Love You by Taking (Not Giving)," *Psychology Today,* May 20, 2011, https://www. psychologytoday.com/blog/the-attraction-doctor/201105/ make-them-love-you-taking-not-giving.

ABOUT THE AUTHOR

Michael Kotick is recognized in the marketing world, having served in leadership roles that range from traditional brand building and business acquisitions to digital marketing strategy. His unconventional and successful marketing initiatives across several brands for Fortune 100 companies (most recently as a Marketing Director at Nestlé) have been featured in *Fast Company, AdAge, AdWeek, e-Marketer,* and more.

www.ingramcontent.com/pod-product-compliance
Lightning Source LLC
Chambersburg PA
CBHW032008170526
45157CB00002B/598